A HISTORY LOVER'S GUIDE TO

OMAHA

A HISTORY LOVER'S GUIDE TO

OMAHA

Eileen Wirth
Carol McCabe

Eileen Wirth and Carol McCabe

The History Press

Published by The History Press
Charleston, SC
www.historypress.com

All photos are courtesy of Omaha Public Library unless otherwise noted.

First published 2021

Manufactured in the United States

ISBN 9781467148450

Library of Congress Control Number: 2021937067

To Omahans, living and dead, who have preserved our city's history and their family histories.

CONTENTS

ACKNOWLEDGEMENTS

Normally we would have a long list of acknowledgements, but this will be short due to researching this book during a pandemic that limited our access to people and places. We hope that despite this major obstacle we have written a book that leads Omahans to explore and better understand their city.

We thank:

Former city planning director Martin "Marty" Shukert for explaining how the city developed and for helping us select the most important buildings to feature. However, any mistakes or misjudgments are ours, not Marty's.

Local history librarians Martha Grenzeback and Lynn Sullivan of the Omaha Public Library, without whose help no one could write any book about local history.

Great Plains Black History Museum director Eric Ewing for his assistance with the North Omaha chapter.

History Nebraska for its website with detailed information about state historical markers.

The Omaha Public Library for its outstanding online local history resources, including photos, and to the Omaha Public Library Foundation that has helped fund their acquisition.

Boys Town and the Nebraska Jewish Historical Society for their assistance.

The authors of books on Omaha history cited in our bibliography.

INTRODUCTION

Omaha's history hasn't always been pretty, but it's far from dull. And there are reminders of it all over the city, especially in the older neighborhoods east of 72nd Street.

This *History Lover's Guide to Omaha* will introduce readers to events and landmarks in those neighborhoods that might surprise even lifelong residents. The guide tells the stories of buildings that people pass without a second glance; the people who built the neighborhoods, parks, churches, cemeteries and so much more; and museums and major landmarks.

Our goal is to both entertain and enlighten you about our local history, which is far richer than you might ever imagine.

QUICK OVERVIEW OF LOCAL HISTORY

Omaha began as a rough village on the western bank of the Missouri River and grew into the region's city after becoming the headquarters of Union Pacific Railroad in 1862. The railroad gave Omaha its identity and led to the founding of South Omaha's massive stockyards and packinghouses that attracted thousands of immigrant workers. Residents bragged about "the smell of money."

Even though that "smell" is gone with the closing of the packinghouses, it helped define Omaha's combination of blue-collar grit with entrepreneurship and wealth that allowed the city to create landmarks ranging from museums,

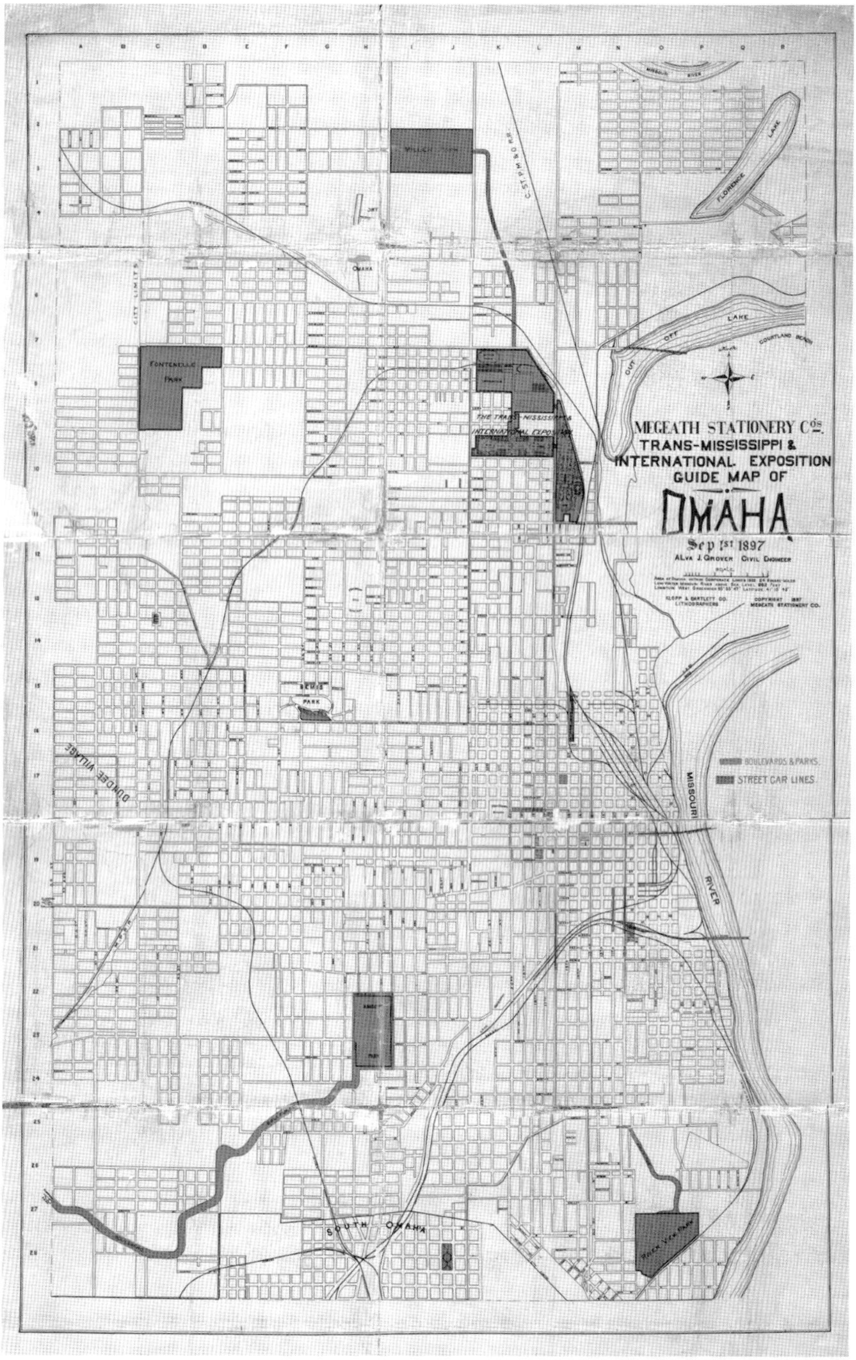

Map of Omaha, 1897.

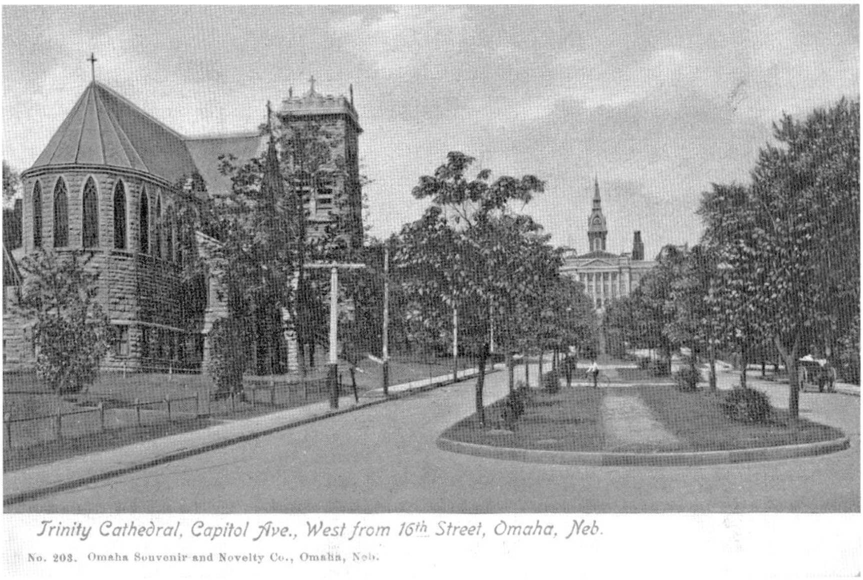

Historic Capitol Avenue and Trinity Cathedral.

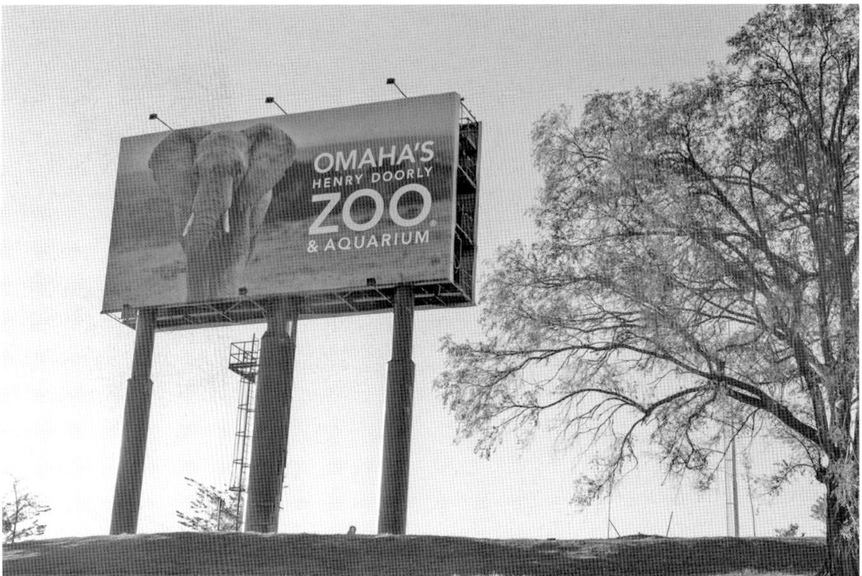

Old Rosenblatt Stadium scoreboard is today's Henry Doorly Zoo billboard. *Photo by Mary Plambeck Cook.*

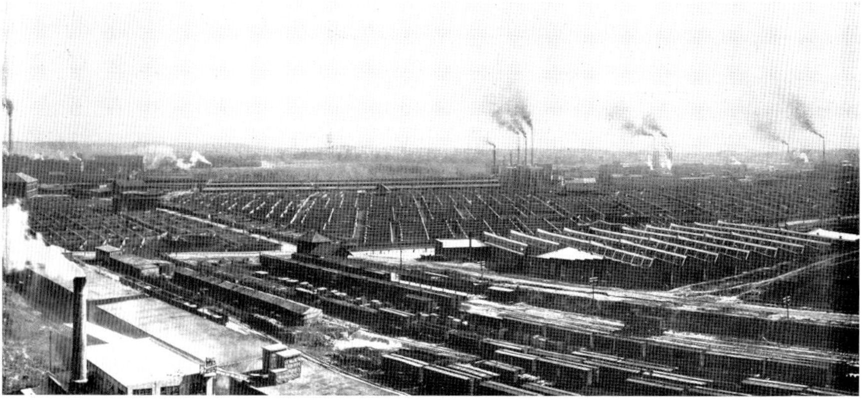

South Omaha's Union Stockyards drew immigrants.

cathedrals and mansions to the world-class Henry Doorly Zoo & Aquarium. Omaha has always been all about making money, whether from meatpacking or high tech.

Get the job done. Make way for progress. If something old gets in the way, tear it down. Only a handful of buildings such as St. Cecilia's Cathedral and Joslyn Art Museum are so historically and artistically important that they are off-limits. There's even a book that tells the story of the historic buildings that Omaha has destroyed.

Omaha's current landscape, especially downtown, is a mixture of historic areas and buildings that have been renovated and reused and new buildings, parks and entertainment venues that have transformed the cityscape. Destruction and creation with renovation when it boosts the local economy—that's the overall story that this *History Lover's Guide to Omaha* tells. Enough reminders of Omaha's past survive to make that story come alive, although often we tell of what *used* to be in a given location.

Come travel through an Omaha you may have thought you knew until viewing it through the lens of the past.

PLAN OF THE BOOK

As noted, we focus on Omaha east of 72nd Street, envisioning the city map as a jigsaw puzzle with eight pieces. Each segment contains at least one major attraction and tells part of the city's story. Our goal is to give you an overall sense of each area and to highlight things to see and do in each. We focus primarily on state historic markers, museums and historic buildings, and locations including homes, churches, cemeteries and parks, and suggest tours through each puzzle piece. We introduce you to numerous buildings and sites but go into detail on only a few. More information is available online for most. We suggest places worth stopping to see. Each tour is designed for about half a day, but that is flexible depending on number of stops.

It should be noted that we researched and wrote this book during the COVID-19 pandemic, when many historic sites, especially museums, were either closed or operating under limited conditions. As this goes to press in 2021, attractions announce changes regularly. Go to websites for current information.

HOW OMAHA DEVELOPED

Thanks to former city planning director Marty Shukert for his insights into how Omaha grew, on which this overview is based. Any errors are ours, not his.

Physically, Omaha began as a village on the west side of the Missouri River and grew north, south and west because it could not grow east. Its explosive growth to the far west began in the modern era and included annexing formerly independent towns such as Millard and Elkhorn, whose history we do not cover. Until the early 1960s, 72nd Street was something of a western boundary, thus it is the western border of this book's focus. We do however include a few important West Omaha locations in one chapter.

Omaha is named for the Omaha Indian Tribe, one of several tribes that the Lewis and Clark Expedition encountered in 1804. Mormons traveling to Utah spent the winters of 1846 and 1847 sheltering at Winter Quarters in today's Florence. However, after that, the federal government forbade white movement into Nebraska until 1854, when Omaha was founded.

Omaha was Nebraska's territorial capital from 1854 until it moved to Lincoln after Nebraska became a state in 1867, but President Lincoln's 1862 decision to name it the eastern terminus of Union Pacific Railroad made Omaha a city. From then on, it would focus on business not government.

The city's original downtown centered on 8th Street from Dodge to Harney Streets. Residential areas grew to the north, south and west. By 1867, Omaha was bounded roughly by the Missouri River, 24th Street, Cuming Street and Pacific Street.

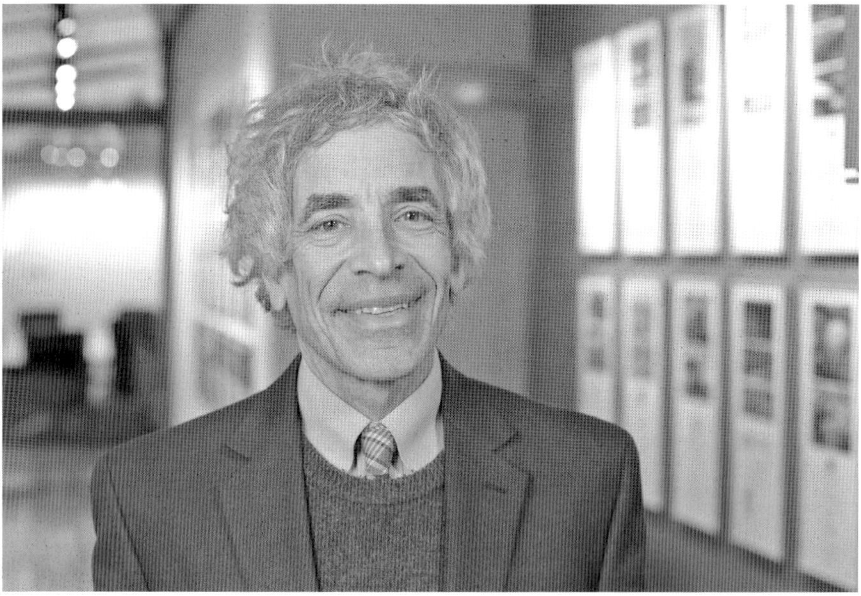

Former city planning director Martin Shukert. *Photo courtesy of Marty Shukert.*

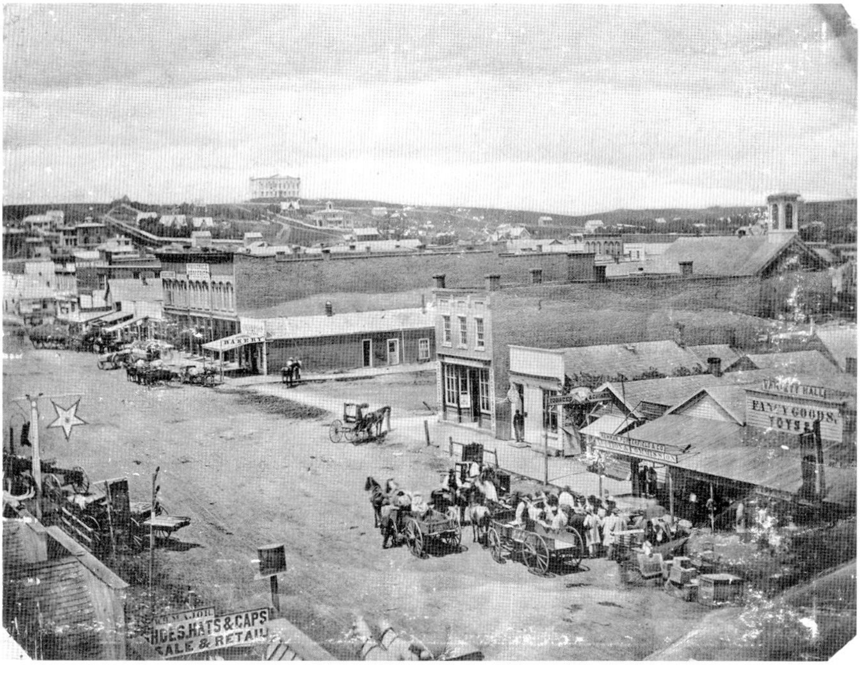

An 1867 view of downtown Omaha's Pioneer Block.

About the same time as Omaha began, Florence was founded on the site of the old Mormon Winter Quarters several miles north of Omaha, and the army directed its war on the Plains Indians from Fort Omaha, then also north of the city. Florence has a treasure-trove of historic sites from the Winter Quarters and territorial eras.

EXPLOSIVE GROWTH IN THE GILDED AGE

During the late 1870s and 1880s, Omaha's population more than doubled as its new stockyards and packinghouses attracted thousands of European immigrant workers. However, the depression of the 1890s devastated the local economy.

Fighting back, business leaders planned the 1898 Trans-Mississippi Exposition, which drew over two million visitors and stimulated the city's cultural development as well as boosting business. Thomas Rogers Kimball, who became the city's leading architect, designed many of the buildings, while Sarah Joslyn's cultural work during the exposition led her to become the era's greatest local arts leader. She later developed and personally paid for Joslyn Art Museum.

Omaha continued growing north, south and west. In downtown, a row of significant commercial buildings was built along Farnam Street, including today's Omaha Building, the first local ten-story building. The 16th Street corridor from Dodge to Leavenworth became the new retail hub and remained so for almost a century, when stores followed the population to new West Omaha neighborhoods. It should be noted that due to Nebraska's annexation law, areas of West Omaha that would be suburbs in many cities have been incorporated in the city.

During the Gilded Age, wealthy Omahans built large homes overlooking the city on the 38th Street ridge stretching from roughly Cuming to Leavenworth in today's Cathedral and Gold Coast areas. Meanwhile, poorer Omahans, including the city's numerous immigrants and minorities, built homes in in lower lying areas in North and South Omaha.

South Omaha City was incorporated in 1886 and grew up around the stockyards and packinghouses. Omaha annexed it in 1915. During the early twentieth century, ethnic groups created distinctive neighborhoods like Little Italy and the African American Near North Side. At the same time, the new streetcar system stimulated the development of western suburban areas and towns, including Hanscom Park, Dundee and Benson, that Omaha long ago annexed.

By the early twentieth century, the footprint of historic Omaha included:

- The downtown business, government and retail hub stretching from the Missouri River to about 24th Street from Dodge to Leavenworth Streets
- South Omaha's stockyards and ethnic neighborhoods
- North Omaha's Florence and African American areas
- Wealthier residential neighborhoods moving west from the Cathedral and Gold Coast neighborhoods.

Within these broad contours are many distinctive smaller districts that paint a picture of the diverse people who laid the foundations of today's city.

We also describe a number of historic sites west of 72nd Street because they tell part of the local historic story.

TOURING SUGGESTIONS

As noted, tours are designed for about half a day except for the Near South segment that includes Omaha's four top tourist destinations: the Henry Doorly Zoo & Aquarium, the Old Market, Lauritzen Gardens and the Durham Museum. We have included at least one major attraction worth touring for half an hour or more in each chapter, and we encourage stops to walk in each. Minus such stops, each segment can be covered in about an hour.

We hope you enjoy these mini vacations within the city.

1
FORT OMAHA AND FLORENCE

Step back into Omaha's pioneer days on this tour of Fort Omaha and Florence. Explore landmarks dating to the Mormon Winter Quarters of 1846–47, Fort Omaha's role in the trial of Ponca chief Standing Bear and Florence's years as an independent town.

Today Fort Omaha is a campus of the Metropolitan Community College, but from 1868 to 1871, it was headquarters of the army's Department of the Platte supervising the war against the Plains Indians. Landmarks include the restored home of General George Crook, commander during Standing Bear's trial, when Indians were considered persons in the eye of the law for the first time. During World War I, Fort Omaha became the army's Balloon School and trained more than sixteen thousand airmen for missions such as forward observations of artillery. During World War II, it housed Italian prisoners of war. After the war, the U.S. Navy used it as a training center for the U.S. Marine reserves before giving Omaha most of the land in 1974.[1]

Twenty blocks north, Florence was built on the site of Winter Quarters, where visitors can tour the Mormon museum and historic cemetery. Entrepreneur James Mitchell founded Florence in 1854, immediately after the opening of the Nebraska Territory, and it was incorporated in 1856. A singing society and brass band were organized in 1857–58. The town also had a short-lived newspaper, the *Courier*, during this era.[2] Historic structures include the Bank of Florence, Florence Mill and Florence Water Works. However, Florence remained a small town until Omaha annexed it when it was going bankrupt in 1917.[3]

Village Became Territorial Capital for a Day

Late in 1854, Florence, then an independent village seven miles north of Omaha, made an unsuccessful bid for the Nebraska territorial capital. Omaha was chosen as the capital after the federal government opened Nebraska to white settlement in 1854 although Florence had a longer history as the site of abandoned Mormon Winter Quarters in the 1840s. But Florence retained its ambition to win the capital. In January 1858, it acted on this goal.

A group of representatives from Nebraska City, Florence and other communities seeking to take the capital from Omaha illegally moved the territorial legislature to Florence following a violent outburst at the territorial capitol. The anti-Omaha dissidents had a majority of the votes present in the legislature to move the capital. However, their plan failed when the territorial governor opposed the move. Omaha remained the territorial capital until it moved to Lincoln after Nebraska gained statehood in 1867.

A plaque on North 30th Street in downtown Florence commemorates the event.

Other historic sites and landmarks on this tour include Notre Dame Academy and Convent, Forest Park Cemetery/Potter's Field, the old Mormon Bridge and Hummel Park. Check websites for more information about which sites are open to the public and during what hours.

SUGGESTED TOUR ROUTE

This sixteen-mile tour route includes navigation directions. The remainder of the chapter gives information on sites, organized by category. Within categories such as state historic markers or landmark buildings, sites are listed by their order in the tour.

1. **Fort Omaha Historic Marker**, 5730 North 30th Street.
2. **General Crook House Historic Marker**, West Road, Metropolitan Community College campus. Turn into the campus and take the street west until you see a sign pointing to the Crook House.

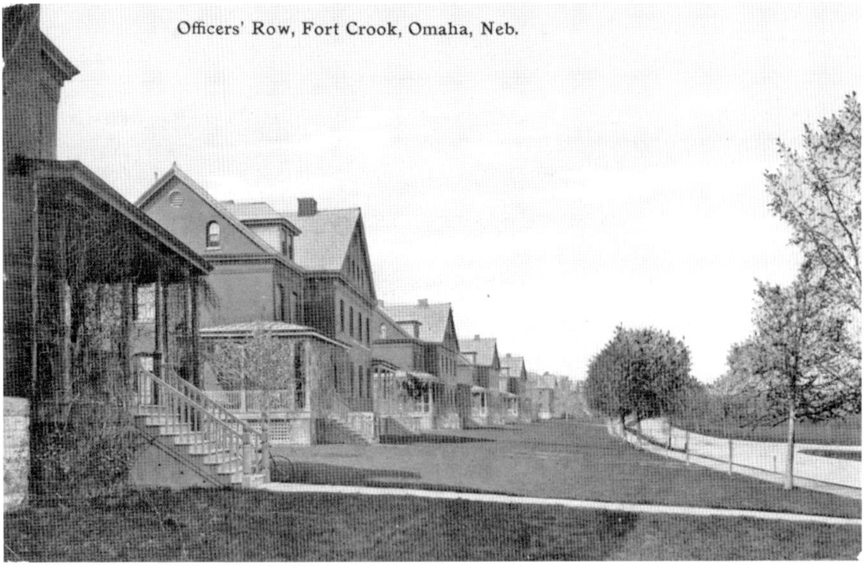

Officers' Row at Fort Omaha.

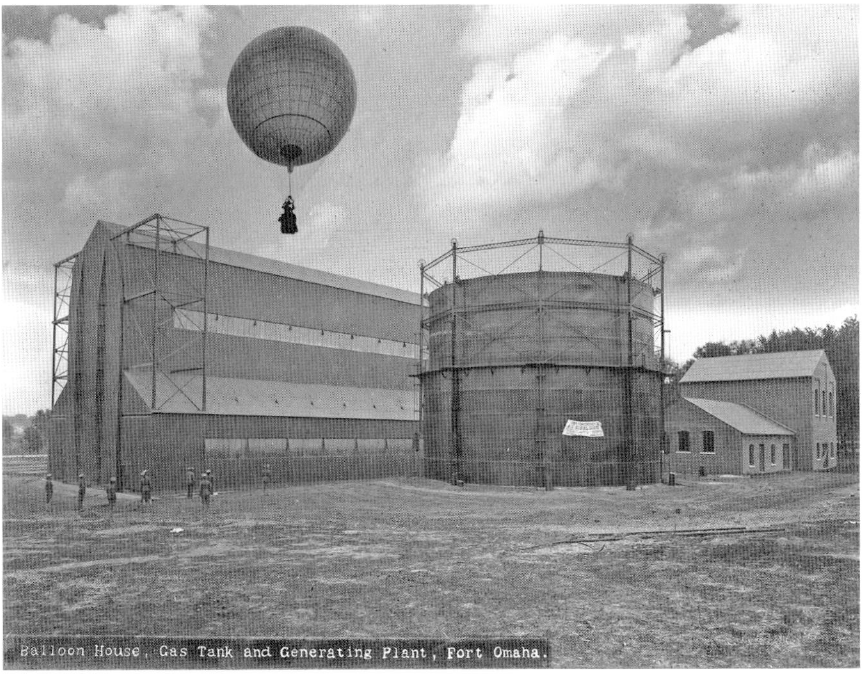

Fort Omaha was Army Balloon School headquarters.

3. **Keirle House**, 3017 Mormon Street. Leave the campus and head north on 30th to Mormon Street. Go one block west. The house is on the south, overlooking Florence Park.
4. **Winter Quarters Historic Marker**, 8300 North 30th Street. In Florence Park facing 30th Street.
5. **Mormon Trail Center and Mormon Pioneer Cemetery**, 3215 State Street. Go west on State Street to the Trail Center historic museum and cemetery. Plan on touring the center and cemetery.
6. **Notre Dame Academy and Convent**, 3501 State Street. Continue west on State Street past this site and continue driving west on State for about five minutes past the south side of Forest Lawn Memorial Park Cemetery and Potter's Field.
7. **Forest Lawn Memorial Park Cemetery and Potter's Field**, Forest Lawn Cemetery Drive. Continue west on State Street to Forest Lawn Cemetery Drive. Turn left and enter the two cemeteries. Potter's Field signs are visible from State Street.
8. **Bank of Florence Historic Marker**, 8502 North 30th Street. Go east on State to 30th and then go north through the historic sites in downtown Florence.
9. **Florence Depot**, 9000 North 30th Street.
10. **Florence Mill Historic Marker**, 9150 North 30th Street.
11. **Mormon Bridge**, across the Missouri River, visible from John Pershing Drive.
12. **Lewis and Clark Campsite Historical Marker**, 12–16 Dodge Park Road is located in Dodge Park (east side of John J. Pershing Drive) near the Dodge Park Marina office.
13. **Hummel Park**, 11808 Pershing Drive.
14. **Florence Water Works**, John J. Pershing Drive. Drive south from Hummel Park and see it on the west side of the road.
15. **John J. Pershing Monument**, 8200 Pershing Drive.

HISTORICAL MARKERS AND LANDMARKS

Nebraska Historical Markers

Fort Omaha

5730 North 30th Street

The fort's military history comes alive in its landmarks, such as the gracious homes built for officers during the years when it was Department of the Platte headquarters. The Standing Bear Memorial is located by the parade ground flagpole. Other buildings at Fort Omaha included a fire station that became a post exchange building, a guard house, a hospital and a Knights of Columbus Assembly Hall that became a Red Cross canteen during World War I.

General George Crook House

W Road, Metropolitan Community College Fort Omaha Campus

This Italianate brick house in the National Register of Historic Places was completed in 1879 as the home of the commander of Fort Omaha. Its first occupant was General George Crook, a noted Indian fighter who sympathized with Ponca chief Standing Bear, who was arrested for returning to Nebraska to bury his son after his tribe had been expelled. Guests at the home included General and Mrs. Ulysses Grant and President Rutherford B. Hayes. The home, which is furnished in period style, is open to visitors.[4] Check the website for hours and for special events held at the home.

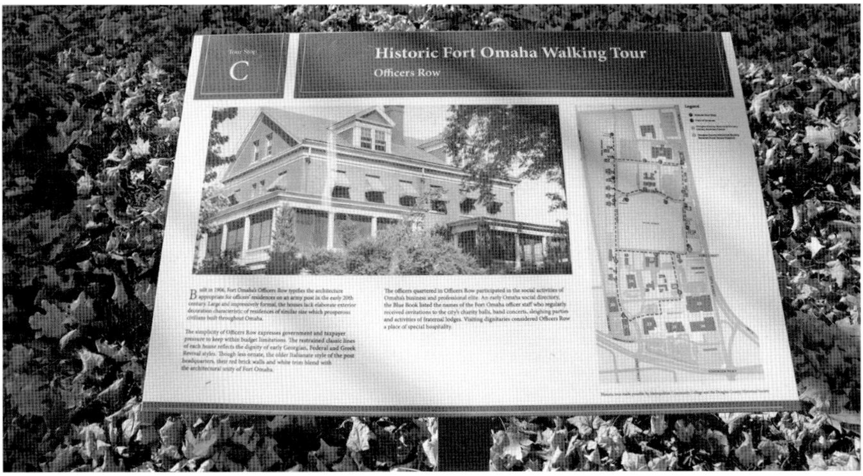

Walking tour sign by Officers' Row. *Photo by Carol McCabe.*

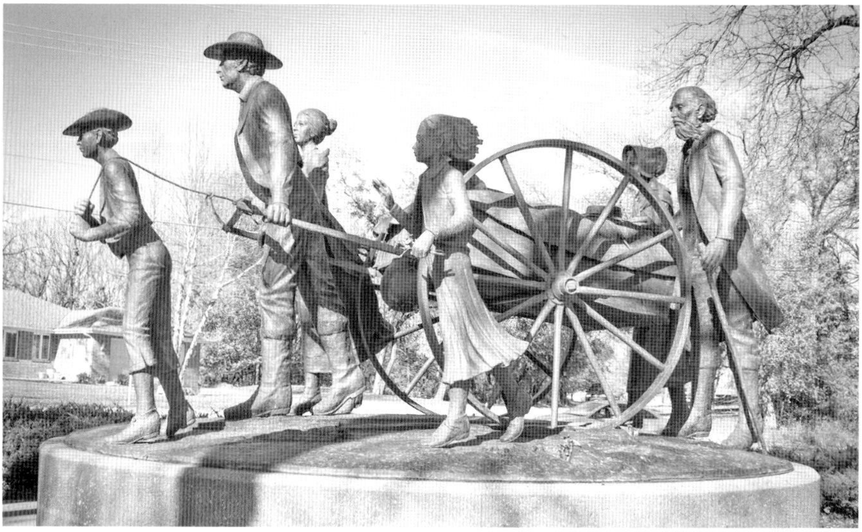

Mormon pioneer statue near the temple at Winter Quarters. *Photo by Carol McCabe.*

Winter Quarters

Florence Park, 8300–8398 North 30th Street

This marker commemorates Florence's Mormon heritage. Historic Winter Quarters is a site on the **Mormon Pioneer National Historic Trail** run by the National Park Service. Attractions include a museum featuring artifacts similar to those the pioneers used, the **Mormon Pioneer Cemetery** containing graves of those who died at Winter Quarters and a famous statue honoring them. In 2001, the Mormon Church dedicated the Winter Quarters Nebraska Temple because of the site's importance in the religion's history.[5]

Forest Lawn Memorial Park Cemetery and Potter's Field

Forest Lawn Cemetery Drive

Forest Lawn Memorial Park Cemetery was established in 1885 and includes the graves of many prominent Omahans as well as veterans from the Civil War and subsequent conflicts. It has been called one of the nation's most beautiful cemeteries.[6]

Potter's Field Cemetery, 5000 Young Street, is adjacent to Forest Lawn and was used to bury poor people or people with no known identity from across the Omaha area. Among those buried there is Will Brown, the prisoner who was lynched in the infamous courthouse riot of 1919. In 1986, a volunteer group restored Potter's Field, and the City of Omaha maintains it.[7] It now has its own state historic marker.

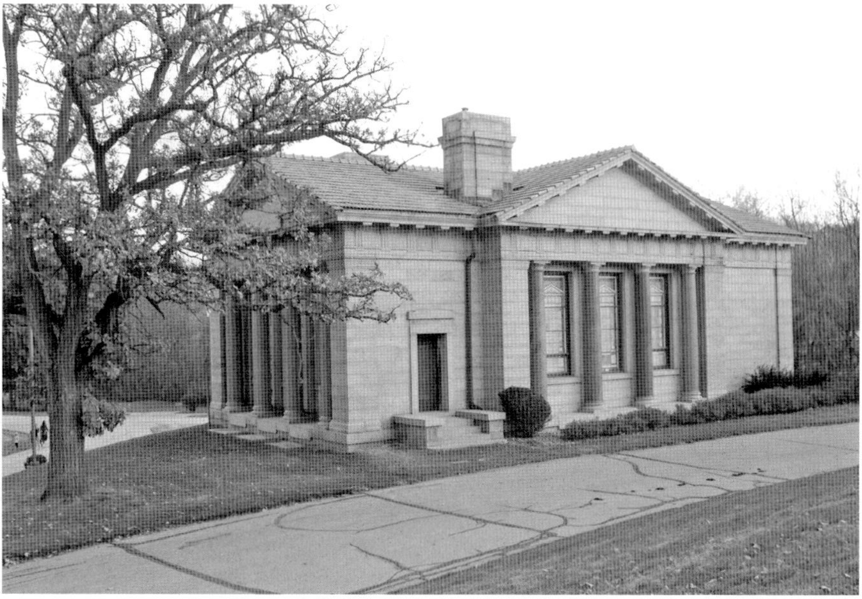

Historic mausoleum at Forest Lawn Cemetery. *Photo by Carol McCabe.*

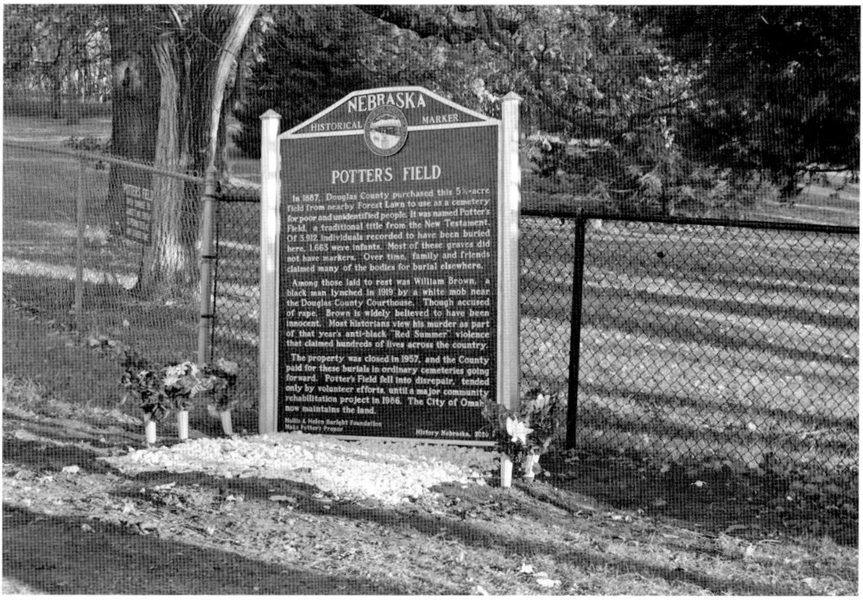

Nebraska historic marker at Potter's Field. *Photo by Carol McCabe.*

Bank of Florence

8502–8508 North 30th Street

The Bank of Florence, which is in the National Register of Historic Buildings, was located in this restored brick building built in 1856. It played an important role in the town's aspirations to become Nebraska's transportation and financial center. After it failed in 1859 due to a financial panic, it housed a variety of businesses, including a second Bank of Florence in 1904.[8]

Florence Mill

9150–9272 North 30th Street

The Mormons constructed this water-powered mill, which is in the National Register of Historic Buildings, during the winter of 1846–47 to supply them with both flour and lumber but abandoned it along with Winter Quarters. In 1856, it reopened to meet the needs of Florence. Flour was its most important product, and by 1880, it had become steam powered. It reflects the important role of the milling industry in developing Nebraska.[9]

Lewis and Clark Campsite—July 27, 1804

12–16 Dodge Park Road

The Lewis and Clark Expedition camped near here at the end of July/early August in 1804. Captain William Clark and Private Reuben Field walked on the Nebraska shore of the Missouri River exploring mounds near where the Oto Indians formerly lived. The mounds might have been natural features. On August 3, the explorers met with leaders of the Oto and Missouria tribes at a site they called Council Bluff near today's Fort Calhoun.[10]

Historic Florence Buildings, Museums and Sites

Besides the buildings already noted, Florence includes other historic structures, some of which are open to the public while others are visible from the street.

Keirle House

3017 Mormon Street

This classic box-style house built in 1905 is designated as an Omaha landmark. It was built by the Keirle family, owner of the Keirle Ice Company, which shipped ice from the Florence Water Works across the Midwest. The house

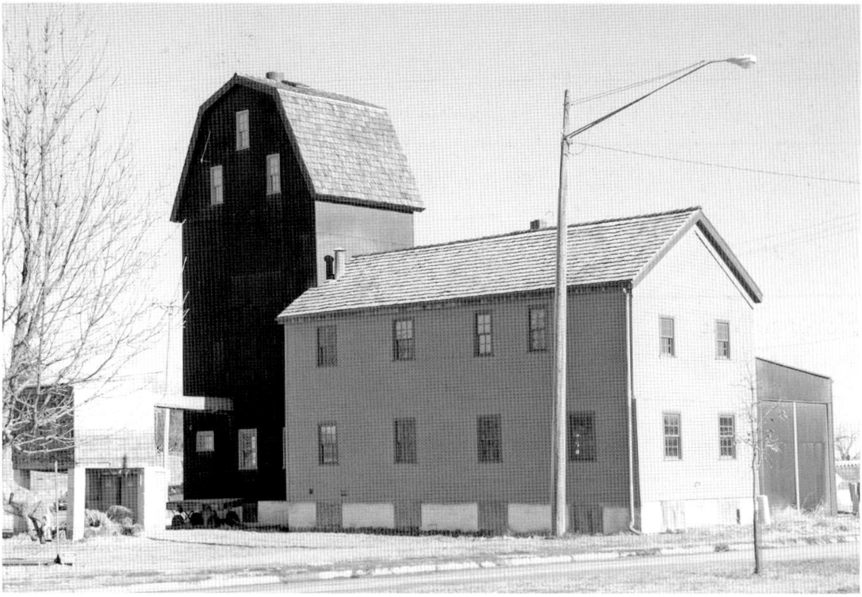

Florence Mill dates to the Winter Quarters era. *Photo by Carol McCabe.*

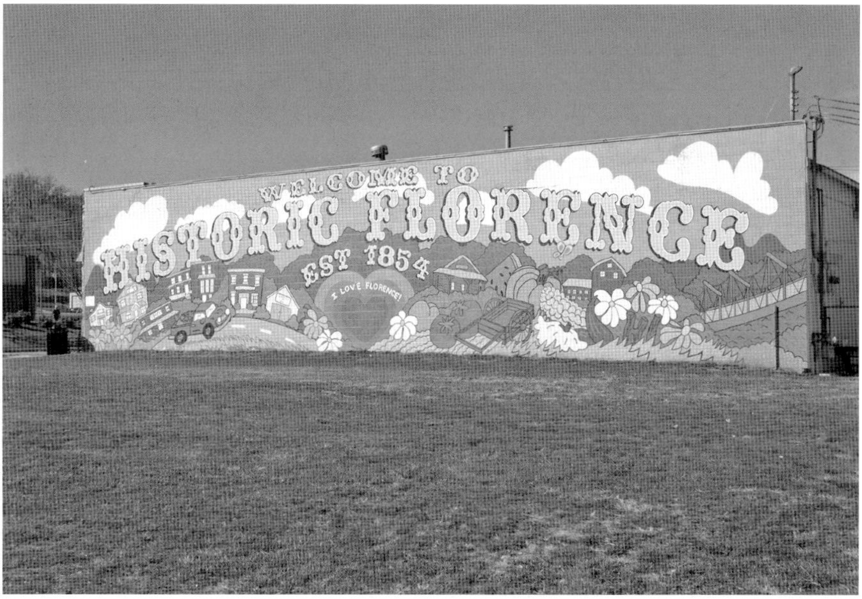

Colorful mural greets visitors to Florence. *Photo by Carol McCabe.*

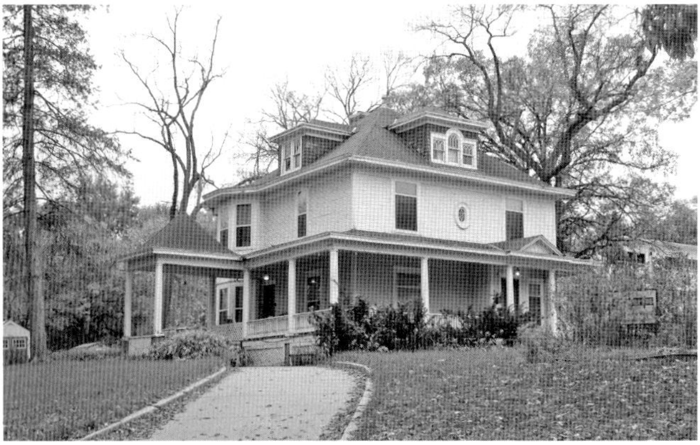

Keirle House in downtown Florence. *Photo by Carol McCabe.*

was built to face the town square of Winter Quarters. In 1996, the Florence Historical Foundation restored the house, which is empty.[11]

Notre Dame Academy and Convent

3501 State Street

This convent and former school for girls is in the National Register of Historic Places and was once called Seven Oaks Farm, an early site of Boys Town. The Czechoslovakian School Sisters of Notre Dame built it in 1926 after coming to the United States to support Czech immigrants. Its Italian Renaissance Revival style was influenced by the Trans-Mississippi Exposition. Formerly, it housed Notre Dame Academy, which closed in 1974. The Sisters of Notre Dame now operate it as Seven Oaks of Florence, housing low-income seniors.[12]

Florence Depot (Museum)

9000 North 30th Street

The depot was built in 1888 as part of a train line from Omaha to Sioux City and was used as a commuter station for passengers, a mail drop-off and a freight depot for bulk cargo such as coal, lumber, stone and ice. Today the Florence Historical Foundation operates it as a small museum featuring exhibits about local railroads. Displays include a caboose and flat car from the 1890s. Check the website for further information on hours and programs.[13]

Mormon Bridge

Missouri River I-80

This bright blue bridge is located at the site of the earliest consistent crossing of the Missouri, dating to 1846 when Mormons operated a ferry here. There were numerous attempts to construct a bridge at the site until this bridge was completed in 1953. To do so, Nebraska created the North Omaha Bridge Commission. Originally, it was a toll bridge. When the second bridge was added on the north, it became part of the Interstate Highway System.[14]

Florence Water Works

John J. Pershing Drive

The City Water Works Company constructed the Florence Water Works in 1880. In 1887, the American Water Works Company purchased it and built the Minne Lusa Pumping Station in 1889. American produced ice from the Missouri River and distributed it throughout the region. In 1913, American refused to sell the water works to the Metropolitan Utilities District (MUD) but lost a court battle. This cost Florence its tax revenue and led to the town's bankruptcy and annexation by Omaha. The Metropolitan Utilities District (MUD) still operates the water works.[15]

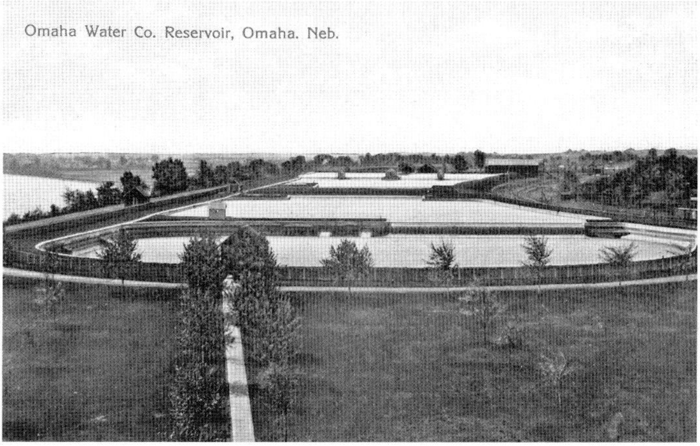

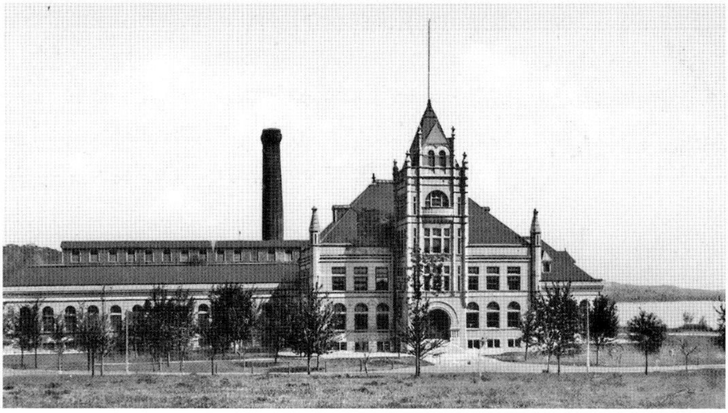

This page: Florence Water Works and Reservoir off Pershing Drive.

John J. Pershing Monument

8200 J.J. Pershing Drive

This small monument honoring General of the Armies John J. Pershing was dedicated in 1941. Early in Pershing's career, he was on the faculty of the University of Nebraska. During World War I, he commanded the American Expeditionary Force. The street also is named in his honor.[16]

Historic Parks

Hummel Park

11808 John J. Pershing Drive

Hummel Park, located north of Florence, was founded in 1930 and is named after Joseph R. Hummel, a longtime superintendent of parks and recreation. This forested area includes the Omaha Riverfront Trail North and other hiking trails. There are horseshoe pits, a Missouri River overlook, a picnic shelter and a disc golf course. The "Devil's Slide" is a natural cliff. The Hummel Park Nature Center offers environmental education and there's also a popular summer day camp.[17]

THINGS TO DO

Every summer, Florence throws the Florence Days festival celebrating its history. It also hosts a popular Farmer's Market. At other times, walk the picturesque commercial district and stop at any of the neighborhood cafés. You can also hike the Hummel Park bluffs or enjoy many activities in Dodge Park. Check websites for information on facilities.

The Douglas County Historical Society, which is next door to the Crook House, holds special events such as its popular Second Sunday lectures which it carries on its website. There are also special events at the Crook House. Check the Crook House website for information such as hours and events.

Enjoy neighborhood cafés for refreshments during your visit.

2
NORTH OMAHA

The Jewell Building, which used to host some of the nation's top Black musical stars, has been renovated and now houses the Great Plains Black History Museum. Nearby, the Union for the Contemporary Arts has converted the Blue Lion Center into an important modern arts cultural center often featuring the work of Black artists. There's even a new version of the old Fair Deal Café, the soul food restaurant called Omaha's Black City Hall during the civil rights era.

In short, there's a lot happening in this historic area that might surprise most Omahans.

North Omaha celebrates its African American history and culture with a variety of sites mostly centered along the North 24th Street commercial area. There are new housing and commercial developments, as well as a few reminders, such as Sacred Heart Catholic Church, that North Omaha was once a center of the Irish community in addition to being an early center of the Jewish community. This area tour also includes landmarks commemorating other significant events, most notably the 1898 Trans-Mississippi Exposition, Omaha's world's fair. The tour begins in Prospect Hill Cemetery, Omaha's oldest, the burial place of notable/notorious residents such as Anna Wilson, the city's leading madam.

But this tour focuses on African American history and culture with small gems like the sculptures of jazz musicians in Dreamland Plaza and the birth site of Malcolm X. Celebrate the neighborhood where some of the nation's greatest athletes, such as hall of famers Bob Gibson and Gale Sayers, grew up.

Robert F. Kennedy's 1968 Campaign Stop

In April 1968, Robert Kennedy concluded his presidential primary campaign trip through Nebraska with a rally at 24th and Erskine Streets in the heart of North Omaha. Photos show a large crowd of enthusiastic Black supporters. Historian Arthur Schlesinger described the event in his iconic biography of Kennedy: "He made his last Nebraska speech in the black section of Omaha. It had begun to pour and the absurdity of it all overcame him. 'Have any of you noticed that it's raining?' he asked. 'Yes,' the crowd—surprisingly large—shouted back. 'If there are silly things to do,' Kennedy said, 'then this is the silliest. It's silly for you to be standing in the rain listening to a politician....As George Bernard Shaw once said, run for the busses.'"

Earlier, at a stop at Creighton University, Kennedy had scolded his mostly white audience for supporting the student draft deferments that allowed them to avoid serving in the Vietnam War. Kennedy asked students at this Catholic university how they could morally accept the fact that the poor, especially Black people, were doing most of the fighting and dying.*

Kennedy won the Nebraska primary about a month before he was assassinated on June 5, 1968.

* Schlesinger, Robert Kennedy, 888–9.

SUGGESTED TOUR ROUTE

This tour route includes navigation directions. The remainder of the chapter gives information on sites. It is organized by category. Within categories such as state historic markers or landmark buildings, sites are listed by their order in the tour.

1. **Historic Prospect Hill Cemetery**, North 32nd and Parker Streets. Take 30th Street to Parker and turn left. Go to 32nd Street. The cemetery is on your right. The historic marker is by the administration building, and the grave of legendary madam Anna Wilson is just off the first road on your left. Note: it is marked "Allen" for her male companion, gambler Dan Allen.

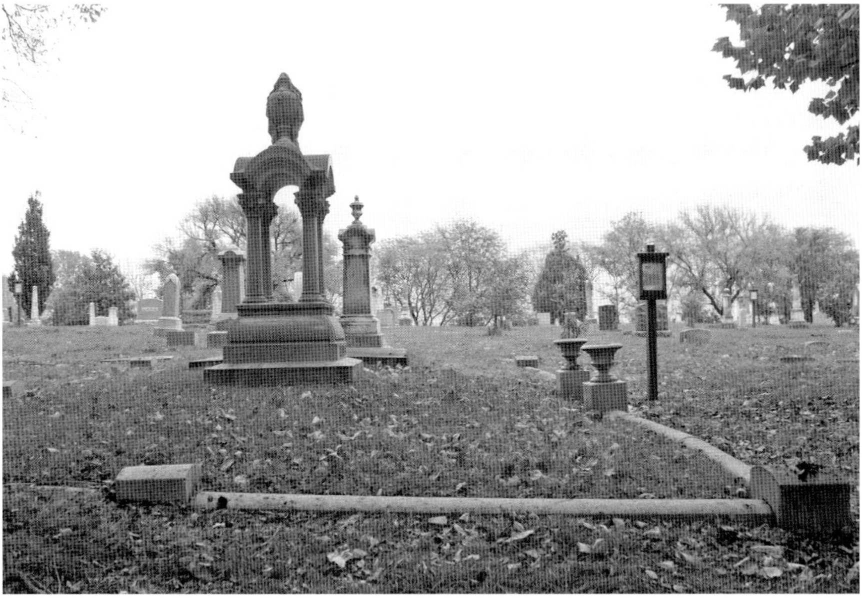

Omaha madam Anna Wilson's grave in Historic Prospect Hill Cemetery. *Photo by Carol Mccabe.*

2. **Carver Savings and Loan Association** and **Martin Luther King Cornerstone Marker**, 24th and Lake Streets. Return to 30th Street and go north to Lake Street. Take Lake to 24th Street. These two sites are next door to each other. The next several stops are all on 24th Street.
3. **Love's Jazz and Art Center**, 2510 North 24th Street.
4. **Union of Contemporary Art**, 2423 North 24th Street.
5. **Dreamland Plaza**, 2322 North 24th Street.
6. **Omaha Star** and **Mildred Brown Park**, 2216 North 24th Street.
7. **Great Plains Black History Museum/Historic Jewell Building**, 2221 North 24th Street.
8. **Fair Deal Village MarketPlace**, 2118 North 24th Street.
9. **Zion Baptist Church**, 2215 Grant Street.
10. After this, go east to 22nd Street and follow it north to see **St. John's AME Church**, 2402 North 22nd Street, and **Sacred Heart Catholic Church**, 2218 Binney Street.
11. **Buffalo Bill at the Trans-Mississippi Exposition Historic Marker** and **Kountze Park**, 3500 Florence Boulevard. Go

east to Florence Boulevard and continue north to the following two sites, which are across the street from each other. Today's Kountze Park at 1920 Pinkney Street was the location of the 1898 Trans-Mississippi Exposition.

12. **Malcolm X Historic Marker and Visitor Center**, 3448 Evans Street. Return to 30th Street and go south onto Evans Street. Turn left and go to 34th Street. Park at the visitor center. The marker is in a field that you can walk to from the parking lot, but it is not visible from Evans Street.

HISTORICAL MARKERS AND LANDMARKS

Nebraska Historical Markers

Historic Prospect Hill Cemetery

Parker Street and North 32nd Street

This pioneer cemetery was founded in 1858 by real estate developer Byron Reed and contains more than fifteen thousand graves, including those of nearly one hundred soldiers killed during the Civil War or while serving at Fort Omaha. Names on tombstones are a veritable who's who of early Omaha. Prospect Hill's most famous grave is that of Anna Wilson, Omaha's top madam, and Dan Allen, her gambler male companion. Mrs. Thomas Kimball, mother of architect Thomas Rogers Kimball, began laying a wreath on Wilson's grave every Memorial Day in honor of her later donations to charities such as the Creche day nursery. Today, that custom has been revived at a popular Prospect Hill Memorial Day ceremony. Thomas Rogers Kimball designed a mausoleum for the Megeath family, which was prominent in both business and politics, and a monument for Senator Joseph Millard's family.[18]

Buffalo Bill at the Trans-Mississippi Exposition of 1898

3500 Florence Boulevard

William F. "Buffalo Bill" Cody held the first official performance of his Wild West show at the Omaha Driving Park near here in 1883. Some eight thousand people attended it. A site at 18th and Sprague Streets later featured a local Wild West show as part of the 1898 Trans-Mississippi Exposition. Cody brought his show back to Omaha for the Trans-Mississippi, and August 31 was designated as Cody Day. The event was so popular that it had to be moved to 20th and Paul Streets to accommodate the crowds. Buffalo Bill's show was seen by millions in twelve countries over thirty years. He died in 1917 and is buried on Lookout Mountain near Denver. Scout's Rest Ranch State Historical Park in North Platte honors him.[19]

Malcolm X Birth Site

3500–3598 North 34th Avenue (34th and Evans)

This site celebrates Omaha's ties to assassinated civil rights legend Malcolm X. He was born as Malcolm Little in 1925 in a house at 3448 Pinkney Street. His family left Omaha a few years later after night riders threatened his father, Reverend Earl Little, for helping organize the Universal Negro Improvement Association. Malcolm converted to Islam and changed his name while in prison. An outspoken opponent of racial discrimination, he counseled the need for human brotherhood after a pilgrimage to Mecca. He was assassinated in New York City in 1965. Rowena Moore, a local civil rights leader whose family owned the house where Malcolm was born, led the fight for this state historical marker, the visitor center and the site's addition to the National Register of Historic Places. The house itself was torn down before 1970.

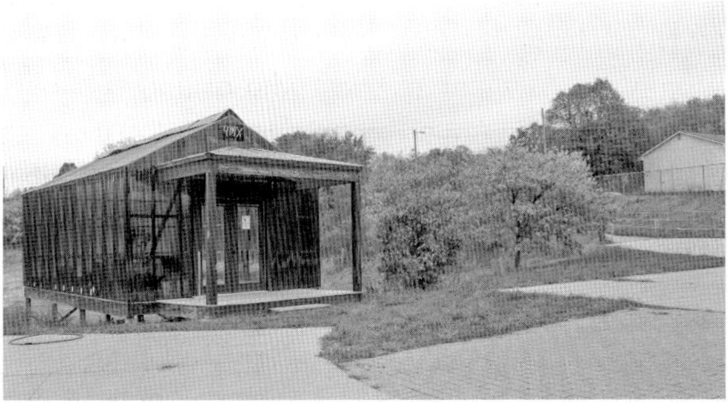

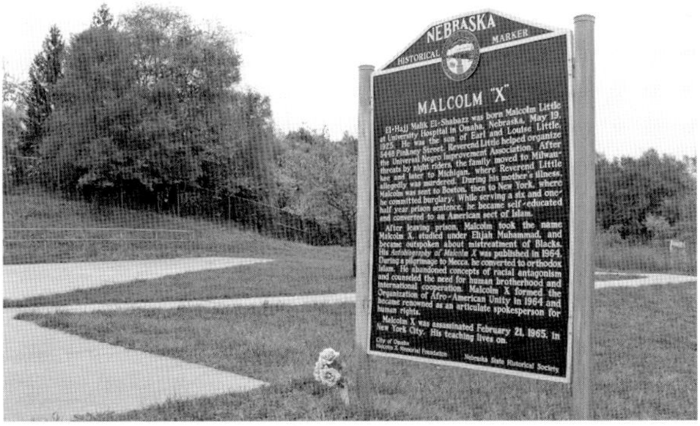

This page: Omaha was the birth site of Black leader Malcolm X. *Photo by Carol McCabe.*

Historic Buildings, Museums and Sites

Carver Savings and Loan Association and Martin Luther King Cornerstone Memorial

24th and Lake Streets

Carver Saving and Loan Association housed Omaha's first Black financial institution and was located in the heart of the Black business district when it opened in 1944.[20] Next door you will see the Martin Luther King Cornerstone Memorial and a building with a colorful wall mural celebrating Black history.

Love's Jazz & Art Center

2510 North 24th Street

This center, named in honor of Omaha jazz great Preston Love, celebrates North Omaha's African American culture and has sponsored cultural events such as Native Omaha Days. It has been closed, but there are plans to reopen it as a music program center. Check online for information on events.[21]

The Union for the Contemporary Arts

2423 North 24th Street

This impressive gallery in the old Blue Lion Building showcases exhibits by Omaha contemporary artists, including Black artists. While technically it is not "historic," it is an important stop on this tour because it is an example of the rebirth of culture and the arts in the North 24th Street historic corridor. Check the website for information on hours and exhibits.

Dreamland Plaza

2322 North 24th Street

The City of Omaha opened the small Dreamland Plaza park in 2003 to pay tribute to North Omaha's jazz history. It is named after the Dreamland Ballroom

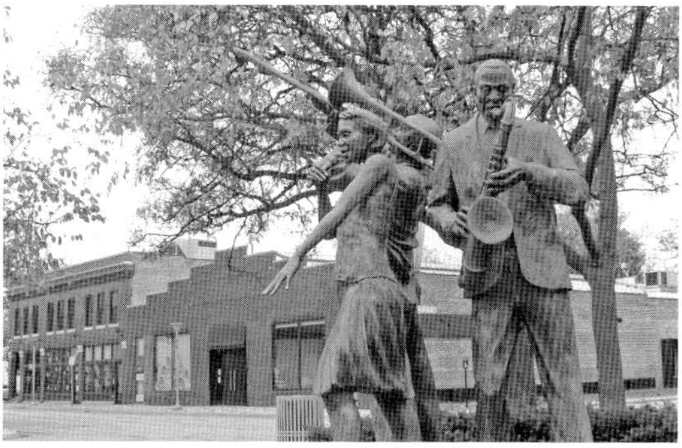

Jazz musician statues in Dreamland Plaza, with Union for the Contemporary Arts in background. *Photo by Carol McCabe.*

and features a nine-foot-tall statue called *Jazz Trio* created by nationally recognized Black sculptor Littleton Alston of Creighton University. The statue depicts a trumpeter, a saxophone player and a female singer performing.[22]

Omaha Star Building and Mildred Brown Park

2216 North 24th Street

The office of Omaha's African American newspaper, Mildred Brown's *Omaha Star*, was built in 1923 and is in the National Register of Historic Places. Brown, one of the few Black female newspaper publishers, was a leader of Omaha's civil rights movement and lived in the building from the paper's founding in 1938 until she died in 1989. The DePorres Club, an early civil rights organization founded by a Creighton Jesuit, Father John Markoe S.J., met there for a time.[23] The park adjacent to the building is named in Brown's honor.

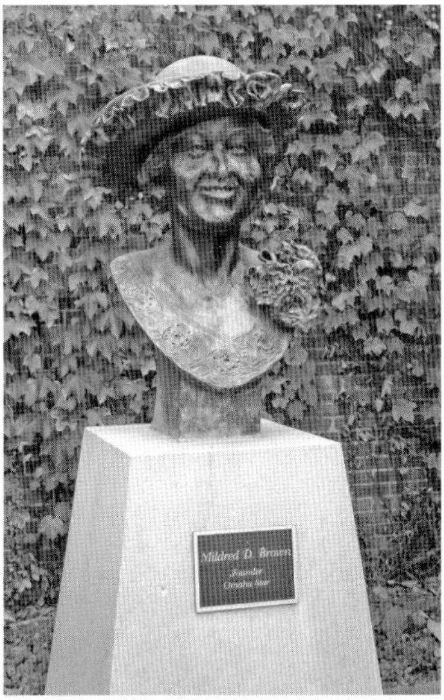

This page: Mildred Brown was the acclaimed publisher of the *Omaha Star* Black newspaper. *Photo by Carol McCabe.*

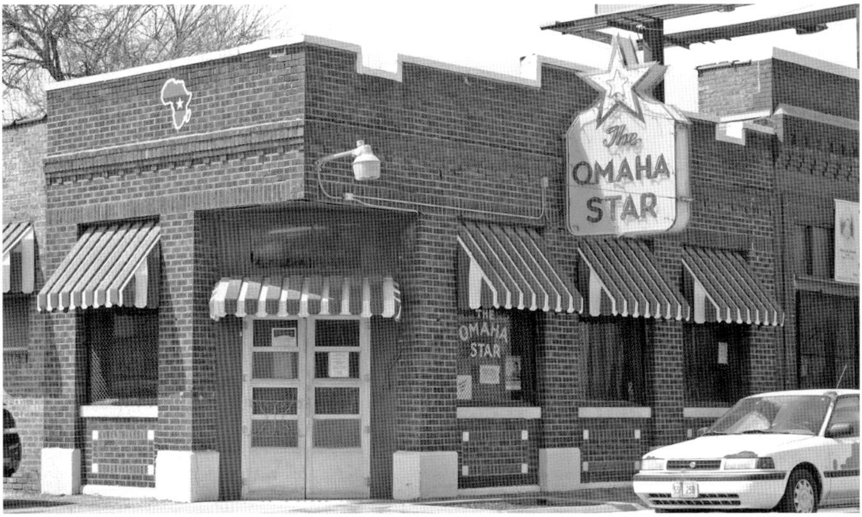

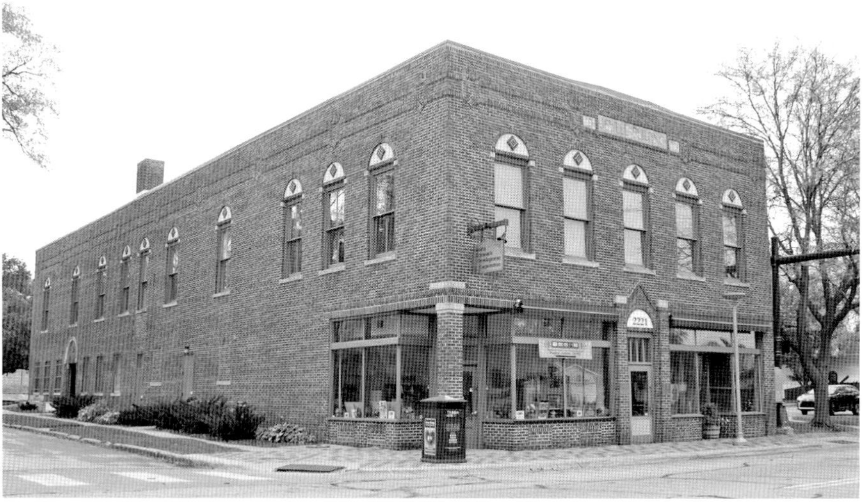

Historic Jewell Building houses today's Great Plains Black History Museum. *Photo by Carol McCabe.*

Great Plains Black History Museum/Jewell Building

2221–2225 North 24th Street

The Great Plains Black History Museum, Nebraska's only Black museum, is located in the historic Jewell Building and celebrates the history of Omaha's African American community. Its permanent collection consists of artifacts gathered mostly by museum founder Bertha Calloway. It also hosts special exhibits. This is the museum's third location since it opened in 1979. Check the Great Plains Black History Museum's website for hours and events.[24]

The Jewell Building

The Jewell Building was built in 1923 in Georgian Revival style, housing a billiard parlor and barbershop on the first floor and the Dreamland Ballroom on the second.

It was built by James Grant Jewell, who had owned a pool hall downtown, and his wife, Cecilia, who had toured Europe as a classical singer. They wanted to give North Omaha a high-class entertainment venue for Black people that that could compete with the Brandeis Ballroom downtown, Krug Park and the Carter Lake Club, all of which occasionally hosted Black performers. The Dreamland Ballroom's height was during the 1930s and 1940s when it was run by James Jewell Jr. The ballroom had a capacity of 400 to 450 but was often packed with crowds of up to 600 for famous big bands and top jazz performers such as Duke Ellington, Louis Armstrong, Ray Charles, Dizzy

Gillespie, Lionel Hampton, Nat King Cole and many others. Count Basie drew the ballroom's largest crowd in 1941.

The ballroom was also the site of major local African American community events and hosted speakers such as James W. Ford, African American Communist Party vice presidential candidate in 1936. During World War II, the federal government took over the ballroom as a USO Club for Black soldiers. Jewell Jr. closed the ballroom in 1965 due to financial problems, although the barbershop remained open until 1975 and the pool hall until 1976.[25]

The Omaha Economic Development Council restored the Jewell Building in the 1980s. It is listed in the National Register of Historic Places and anchors the 24th and Lake Streets Historic District.[26]

Fair Deal Village Market Place

2118 North 24th Street

This modern commercial development on the site of the historic Fair Deal Café includes a reinvented café, Fair Deal Grocery Market and other stores. The original Fair Deal Café was noted for its soul food and was so popular with political and civil rights leaders from the 1940s to the 1970s that it was called Omaha's Black City Hall. The $2.4 million project was locally designed by Alley Poyner Macchietto architectural firm. It opened in 2017.[27]

Zion Baptist Church

2215 Grant Street

Omaha's first Black architect, Clarence W. Wigington, designed this historic church. He began his career working for Thomas Rogers Kimball, who designed St. Cecilia's Cathedral. Wigington also won an art contest at the 1898 Trans-Mississippi Exposition.[28]

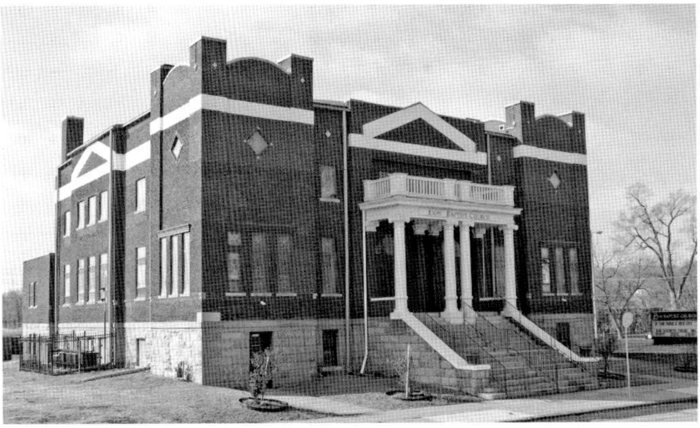

Omaha's first Black architect, Clarence Wigington, designed Zion Baptist Church. *Photo by Carol McCabe.*

St. John's AME Church

2402 North 22nd Street

St. John's AME, organized in 1867, is Omaha's oldest Black congregation. It moved to its current location in 1922 and is in the National Register of Historic Places as an example of Prairie School architecture.[29]

Sacred Heart Catholic Church

2218 Binney Street

Construction of this Gothic Revival stone church began in 1900 to serve Omaha's growing Irish Catholic population. It is noted for its 124-foot spire and is in the National Register of Historic Places. When it was completed, wealthy Catholics built large homes in the parish.[30]

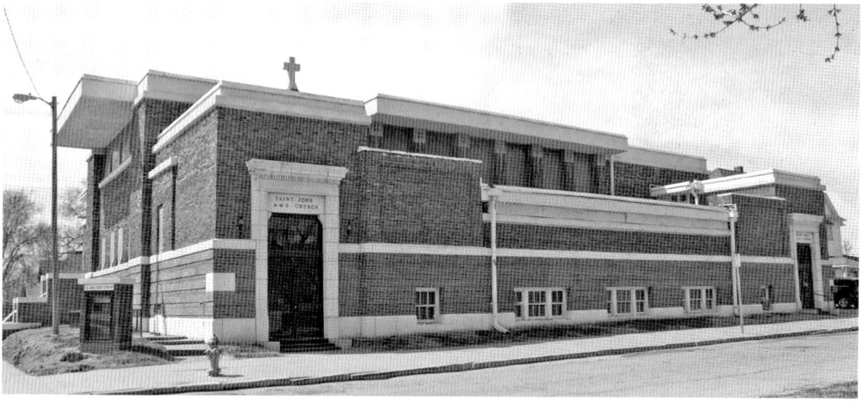

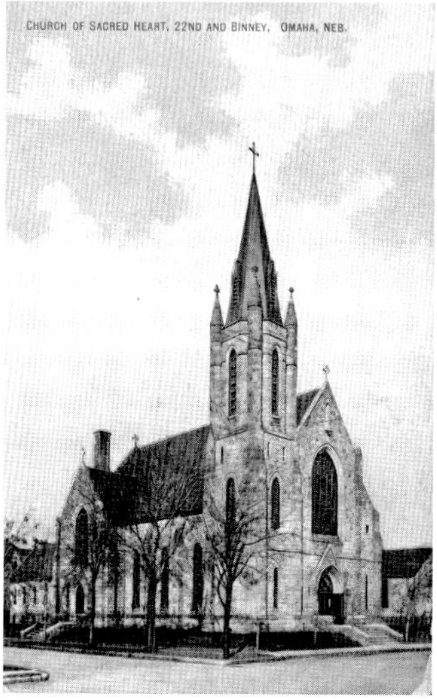

Above: St. John's AME Church is in the National Register of Historic Places, while Sacred Heart Catholic Church was an early Irish parish. *Photo by Carol McCabe.*

Left: Sacred Heart Church.

Historic Parks

Kountze Park

1920 Pinkney Street

This city park was the site of the 1898 Trans-Mississippi Exposition, Omaha's world's fair that drew two million people, including President William McKinley. Where once there was the Grand Court and a lagoon, visitors today will find a water park, a playground, basketball and tennis courts and a pavilion. The park is named for banker Herman Kountze, an important early business leader, and was part of a plot that he owned.[31]

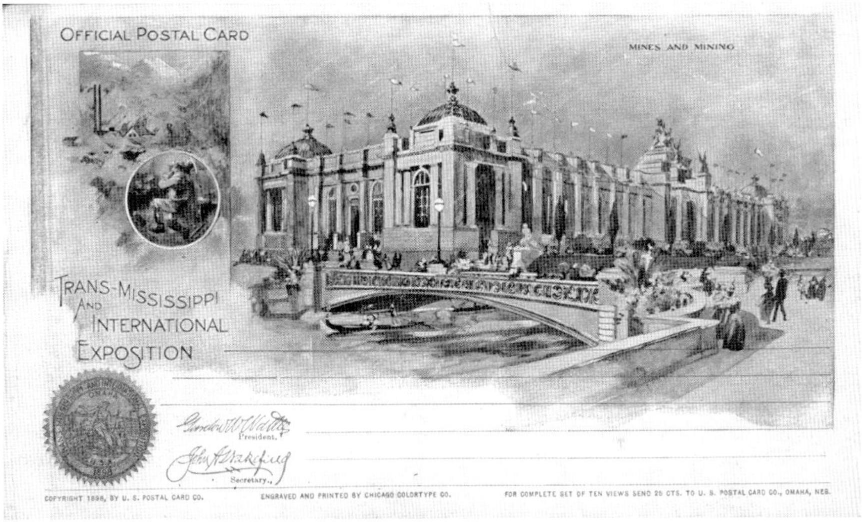

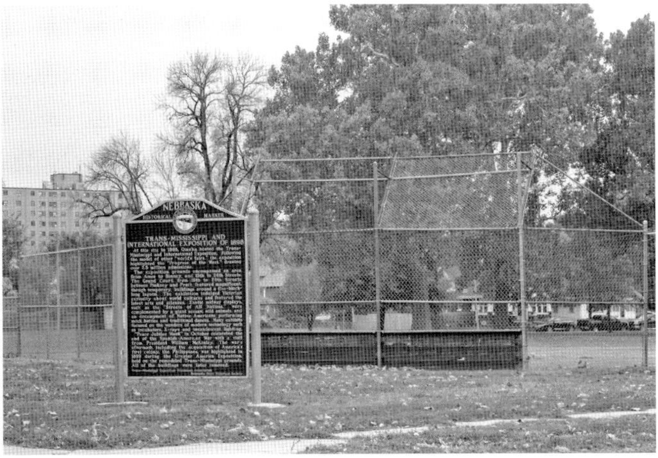

This page: Grounds of the 1898 Trans-Mississippi Exposition became Kountze Park. *Photo by Carol McCabe.*

THINGS TO DO

North Omaha boasts of numerous small restaurants celebrating its culinary heritage, such as the revived Fair Deal Café. There's also the legendary Skeets BBQ at 2201 North 24th Street, Time Out Chicken at 30th and Evans (near the Malcolm X birth site) and others. The Highland Accelerator at 2112 North 30th Street, a major new development, features Hardy Coffee Co. with pastry and Big Mama's Kitchen and Catering, which has been featured on the Food Network for its soul food.

3

DOWNTOWN OMAHA

From pioneer days to the present, downtown Omaha has been both the heart of the city and in a constant state of flux. Today, it's an interesting mixture of renovated landmarks and modern attractions along the riverfront that have reshaped the skyline. Old warehouses in the riverfront district have been transformed into upscale condominiums that fuel the vibe that has turned downtown into a lively residential neighborhood for young professionals and retirees.

This area celebrates its historic treasures like the Orpheum Theater and Central High by continually updating them for the next generation. New skyscrapers like First National Bank incorporate elements of the buildings they replaced or showcase sculptures celebrating Omaha's frontier heritage.

As you traverse the streets on this compact tour, try to imagine an Omaha where 16th Street was the city's retail center and notice the lovely architectural details on such classic buildings as the old main Brandeis Store, now mostly condos, and the old main library, now offices. See how downtown Omaha blends old and new as it thrives as the city's center of the arts, entertainment, business and government although retail has largely moved elsewhere.

Savor the attractions in today's downtown, from top concerts and sports events at the CHI Center or Holland Center to major exhibits at Joslyn Art Museum. Although Omaha has expanded many miles west, its constantly evolving original core remains crucial to its identity.

Golden Spike Days Celebration in 1939

In late April 1939, Omaha celebrated its Union Pacific Railroad heritage with one of the largest festivals in the city's history—Golden Spike Days. The event commemorated the seventieth anniversary of the driving of the Golden Spike on May 10, 1869, in Promontory, Utah, which completed the nation's first transcontinental railroad.

But Golden Spike Days was more of a festival than a history lesson, complete with Hollywood stars coming to Omaha for the premiere of Cecil B. DeMille's movie *Union Pacific* at the Orpheum Theater and Paramount movie theaters. The center of the action was downtown, where the railroad has always been headquartered. President Franklin Roosevelt opened the festivities by pressing a telegraph key at the White House.

The movie's stars participated in a massive parade through downtown, which residents remembered for life. DeMille even borrowed the actual Golden Spike from Stanford University, where it is housed, for the movie's closing scene. However, he used a prop spike for the hammering sequence.

The real Golden Spike was among the artifacts displayed at the Golden Spike Historical Exposition at the Omaha Municipal Auditorium. A quarter of a million people, equal to Omaha's population at the time, attended the exhibit.

To this day, Golden Spike Days remains one of the most notable events in downtown Omaha's history.* The Golden Spike Monument near Union Pacific's main local railyard in Council Bluffs dates to Golden Spike Days.

* "Golden Spike," Wikipedia.

SUGGESTED TOUR ROUTE

This tour route includes navigation directions. The remainder of the chapter gives information on sites, organized by category. Within categories such as state historic markers or landmark buildings, sites are listed by their order in the tour. The directions mention some of the major buildings you will pass, but numerous others line the streets. In addition, the tour, which begins north of downtown at Lewis and Clark Landing, focuses on the abundance of historic landmarks while omitting the key modern components of downtown, such as the CHI and Holland Centers and T.D. Ameritrade Park.

1. **Lewis and Clark Landing/National Park Regional Headquarters and Visitor Center**, 345 Riverfront Drive. Turn south off Abbott Drive onto Riverfront Drive and go south to the site on the east side of the road and turn in.
2. **Trans-Mississippi and International Exposition of 1898 Marker**, Heartland of America Park. Continue driving south along Riverfront Drive into Heartland of America Park. To exit the park, take Riverfront Drive north to 8th Street. Follow 8th north to Capitol Avenue. Go west on Capitol past the modern Capitol District and Omaha World-Herald Freedom Center.
3. **First National's Spirit of Nebraska's Wilderness and Pioneer Courage Park**, 1400 Capitol Avenue and 1601 Dodge Street. This sculpture park celebrating Nebraska's frontier heritage is on the north side of Capitol Avenue with another collection of sculptures on the plaza in front of First National Bank headquarters at 16th and Dodge. Continue west on Capitol.
4. **Trinity Episcopal Cathedral**, 113 North 18th Street. Trinity Episcopal Cathedral is on the north side of Capitol. Turn south on 18th Street and go a block to Dodge Street. **St. Mary Magdalene Catholic Church** is on the south side of the street at 19th. Continue west on Dodge.
5. **Central High School**, 20th and Dodge Streets. Central High, on the north side of Dodge, was originally called Omaha High School and was built on the site of the second territorial capitol building. The grounds include two state historic markers as well as a new arts center.
6. At 20th Street, turn south and pass the **Scottish Rite Cathedral**, 202 South 20th Street, and the **Rose Blumkin Performing Arts Center**, 2001 Farnam (consider stopping). Continue south to Harney Street and turn east, passing **Omaha Library Plaza**, 1823 Harney Street, the former main Omaha Public Library. The back of the **Omaha-Douglas Civic Center** and the **Douglas County Courthouse** are on the north side of the street. At 17th Street, go to St. Mary's Avenue, passing the **Flatiron** building at 1722 St. Mary's Avenue, and

go to Jackson Street past the **Magnolia Hotel**. Turn east and go one block to 16th Street and turn north past the **Orpheum Theater** at 409 South 16th Street and the **Brandeis**, 210 South 16th Street. Turn west onto Farnam Street.

7. **The Omaha Building**, 1650 Farnam Street. This large red stone building is on the north side of the street and the lobby displays an art collection that is open to the public. Drive west on Farnam to the **Douglas County Courthouse** at 1701 Farnam Street. Continue west on Farnam to 19th Street and take it north to Dodge. Turn left onto Dodge Street and go west.
8. **Joslyn Art Museum**, 2200 Dodge Street. Go west on Dodge to 24th Street and go north a couple of blocks to turn into the parking area. The museum's sculpture garden is on the east, along with the major visitor entrance. This major stop concludes the tour.

HISTORICAL MARKERS AND LANDMARKS

Nebraska Historical Markers

Captain William Clark and Private Reuben Field

601 Riverfront Drive

In July 1804, as the Lewis and Clark Expedition traveled up the Missouri, Captain William Clark took Private Reuben Field to explore some mounds on the Nebraska side of the river. The mounds in today's downtown Omaha might have been the remains of the earth lodges where Oto Indians lived, or they might have been natural. Lewis and Clark camped near today's Eppley Airfield. On August 3, they met with the Oto and Missouria Indians at a site they called "Council Bluff" near today's Fort Calhoun.[32]

Trans-Mississippi and International Exposition of 1898

Heartland of America Park

This marker commemorates Omaha's world's fair despite the fact that the exposition was held at today's Kountze Park at 1920 Pinkney Street. The fair was organized to promote and showcase Omaha's recovery from the devastating crash of the early 1890s. It attracted 2.5 million visitors, including President William McKinley, and featured exhibits and cultural events illustrating the "Progress of the West." The grounds were centered on a lagoon, and the Grand Court was lined with monumental temporary buildings designed by architects C. Howard Walker and Thomas R. Kimball. There also was an Indian encampment showcasing the lifestyles of numerous tribes. The exposition helped propel Omaha's development as a progressive commercial center and is one of the most significant events in the city's history.[33]

Central High School

20th and Dodge Streets

Today's Central High School, originally known as Omaha High School, was founded in 1859 and located in Nebraska's first territorial capitol at 9th and Douglas Streets. The territory later built a new capitol on the site of today's high school. When Nebraska moved the capital to Lincoln after statehood, it donated that building to Omaha for educational purposes. Since that building was unsafe, it was replaced with a redbrick school in 1872 that included both high school and elementary classrooms. Omaha High graduated its first class in 1872, but the building could not accommodate both the high school and Central Grade School. The new/current building, built in segments around the old, was completed in 1912. A courtyard occupied the space of the old building. Central High has expanded over the years, including recent additions such as a football stadium and fine arts wing. Its graduates include financier Warren Buffett and two Nobel Prize winners.[34]

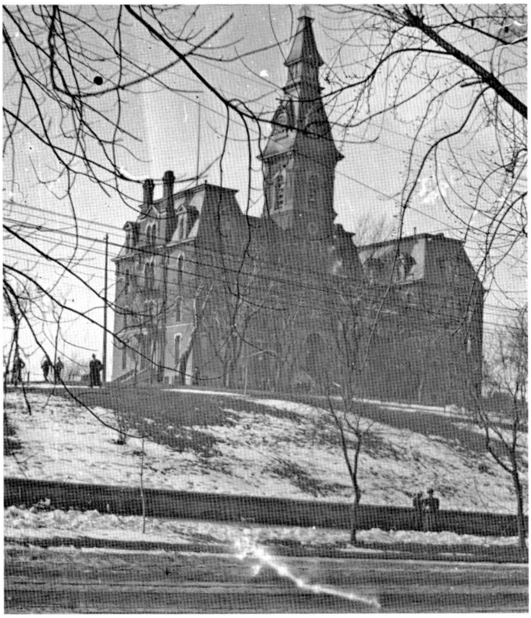

The old Omaha High School was replaced by today's Central High.

Capitol Hill

20th and Dodge Streets

This was the site of Nebraska's second territorial capitol building, housing its government offices from 1857–8 to 1868, when the state capital moved to Lincoln. The handsome brick capitol building that stood on this hill housed the legislature, governor's office, state supreme court and government offices. The state donated the building and site to Omaha for educational purposes, but the building was declared unsafe, and a new school building was built, later replaced by today's building. Central High's central courtyard covers the approximate area of the old capitol.[35]

William Henry Jackson

14th and Douglas Streets

Renowned photographer, artist and explorer William Henry Jackson, who said in 1869 that Omaha had the vitality of a "boomtown," had his first photo studio on this site from 1867 to 1869. Jackson is noted for his photos and sketches of the landscapes of the nineteenth-century West, including scenes from the infant towns along Union Pacific Railroad. He first crossed into Nebraska in 1866 while working as a bullwhacker on the Oregon Trail. His photos of the Yellowstone region contributed to the establishment of the first national park.[36] This marker by the W. Dale Clark Library at 215 South 15th Street is not part of the tour route but is easy to find.

Museums

Joslyn Art Museum

2200 Dodge Street

Joslyn Art Museum, Omaha's principal fine arts museum, was Sarah Joslyn's gift to Omaha that she financed and built as a memorial to her husband, George, who earned a fortune in publishing. This pink marble Art Deco building, designed by Omaha architects John and Alan McDonald, opened in 1931. Its interior features thirty-eight different marbles from all over the world. The elegant interior fountain court inside the main entrance is frequently used for social events. The museum's theater hosts concerts, lectures and other performances. A major modern addition on the building's west end includes a glass atrium containing a gift shop and public cafeteria. Dale Chihuly's glass sculpture *Inside and Out* is on display. The new wing hosts traveling shows and special exhibits.

Joslyn's permanent collection includes works by nineteenth- and twentieth-century American and European artists such as Pierre-Auguste Renoir and artworks showcasing the American West such as the Karl Bodmer collection depicting Native American life before white settlement. Masters represented in its collection include El Greco and Titian. In 2009, Joslyn opened a sculpture garden featuring works by local and national artists as well as a reflecting pool and waterfall. Admission is free. Check the website for hours and information on exhibits and special events.[37]

Historic Buildings

Forty-three downtown buildings are in the National Register of Historic Buildings, but some notable structures such as Joslyn Art Museum aren't on the list. Many are open to the public, while some, such as the old Downtown Brandeis store, are partially open with a street-level café and upscale housing in upper levels.

Trinity Episcopal Cathedral

113 North 18th Street

Construction of this gray stone late Gothic Revival cathedral began in 1880, but the congregation, one of the first in Omaha, is much older. The cathedral features interior Gothic design, including a carved oak bishop's throne and bishop's stall. When the building was dedicated, Omaha historian Alfred Sorensen called it "one of the handsomest church edifices in the west." The stained-glass windows with their stone tracery are particularly beautiful. Bishop

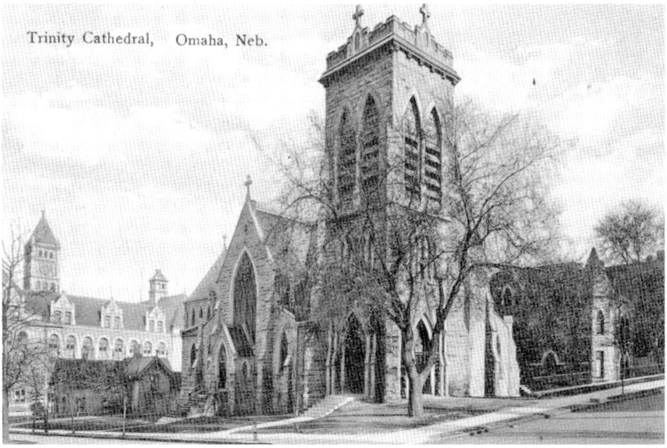

Trinity Episcopal Cathedral is one of Omaha's oldest congregations.

Robert Clarkson and his wife, Meliora Clarkson, are buried in the courtyard. Bishop Clarkson oversaw the building of Trinity Cathedral and founded more than fifty churches. His wife helped found Clarkson Memorial Hospital, which is now part of the University of Nebraska Medical Center.[38]

St. Mary Magdalene Catholic Church

109 South 19th Street

The original St. Mary Magdalene's was built in 1868 by German Catholics and was sometimes called the "Doll Church" because of its size. It was destroyed by a fire in 1894. Another church was built but sold before the current church opened in 1903. In 1919, when Omaha cut down the steepness of Dodge Street to accommodate traffic, a main entrance to the church was left high above street level, and the church had to be rebuilt. That old entrance can still be seen from Dodge.[39]

Scottish Rite Cathedral

202 South 20th Street

The Scottish Rite Cathedral is a Masonic building designed by Omaha architect John Latenser Sr. that opened in 1914. The cathedral, which is in the National Register of Historic Places, uses Ionic columns as part of its classical Greek design because of their significance in Masonic symbolism. During the 1930s, Latenser's firm was the leading one in downtown Omaha, with eighty-nine of ninety-eight blocks containing at least one of its buildings. The cathedral is evidence of the prominence of Freemasonry in Omaha business and governmental leadership.[40]

Omaha Library Plaza

1823 Harney Street

Omaha architect Thomas Rogers Kimball designed the original Omaha Public Library, which is now an office building. This Second Renaissance Revival stone structure opened in 1894 and is listed in the National Register of Historic Places. It is similar in design to the Boston Public Library and remained Omaha's main library until 1978. Drawings of the building were displayed at Chicago's Columbian World's Fair in 1893. The main entrance is noted for its wrought-iron fan light above the door and its ten bas-relief rondels of ancient philosophers, poets and artists such as Plato, Aristotle and Socrates. Local historian Joan Fogarty notes that the building announced "the city's ambition to step forward into a new era of progress and cultural advancement."[41]

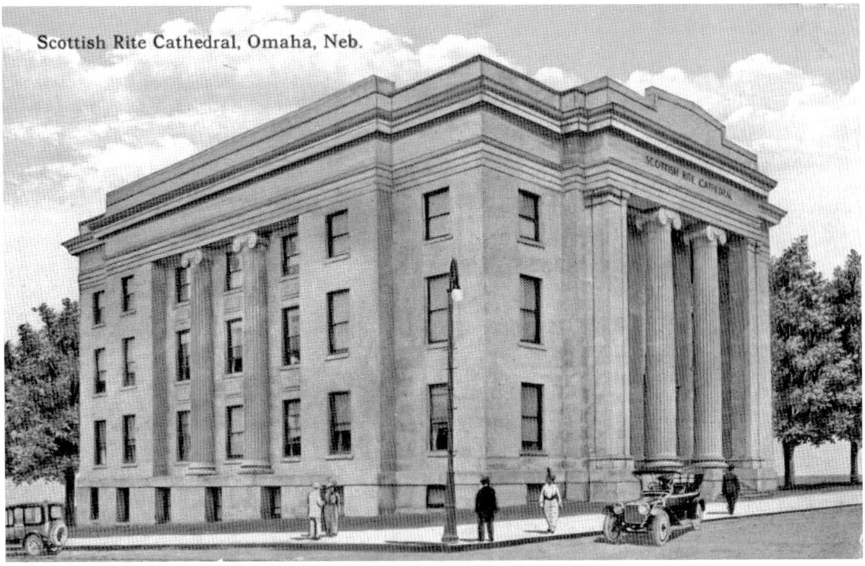

Scottish Rite Cathedral.

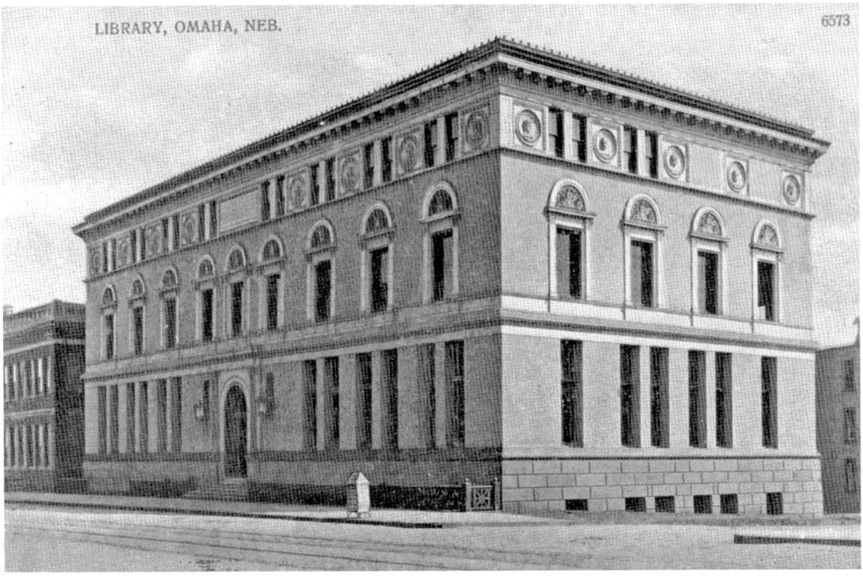

Former downtown library is an office building.

Flatiron

1722 St. Mary's Avenue

Until the COVID-19 pandemic forced its closing in 2020, this distinctive 1912 Georgian Revival building in the National Register of Historic Places housed an upscale continental restaurant, the Flatiron Café. Previously, it had been a hotel used by, among others, 1930s mobsters including Al Capone. The Jamrozy family renovated the building and opened the Flatiron Café in 1995.[42]

Magnolia Hotel

1615 Howard Street

This elegant hotel, formerly known as the Aquila Court Building and before that as the Sheraton Omaha, was built in 1923 and is in the National Register of Historic Places. It was built in a *U* shape, designed after the Bargello in Italy. Originally, it featured an interior courtyard garden that resembled a formal Italian garden. However, the garden was removed during a 1972 renovation that substituted marble slabs and fountains. The Magnolia Hotels purchased Aquila Court in 2006, and it is considered one of Omaha's finest hotels. It includes a public bar/coffee shop.[43]

Orpheum Theater

409 South 16th Street

The Orpheum Theater is one of Omaha's premier live performance venues, hosting touring Broadway shows, concerts and other events. The 2,600-seat proscenium theater was built in 1927 and is listed in the National Register of Historic Places. It was built as a replacement for the old Creighton Theater and added to the Orpheum Circuit, which included nine western cities. In the 1940s, it became a movie theater, gradually deteriorating. In 1975, it underwent a $2 million renovation to restore its Italianate architecture, which includes magnificent crystal chandeliers and elegant staircases. Omaha native Henry Fonda performed as Clarence Darrow in the theater's reopening event.

In 2002, after Omaha Performing Arts took over management of the theater from the city, it underwent another $10 million renovation that allowed it to handle complicated scenery for touring productions such as *The Lion King*. In 2017, a $3 million update improved painting, carpeting and seating. Other improvements include the Orpheum Theater Skylink added in 2004, which connects the theater to the OPPD garage, and the digital electronic display board and the installation of LED posters in the lobby in 2013. The theater boasts a Wurlitzer organ.[44]

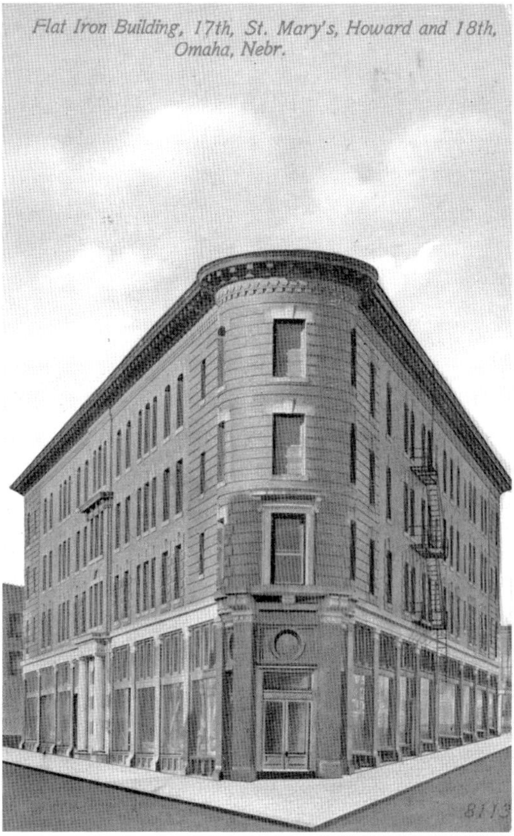

Left: Flatiron Building housed a now-closed fine dining restaurant.

Below: Orpheum Theater has been renovated several times.

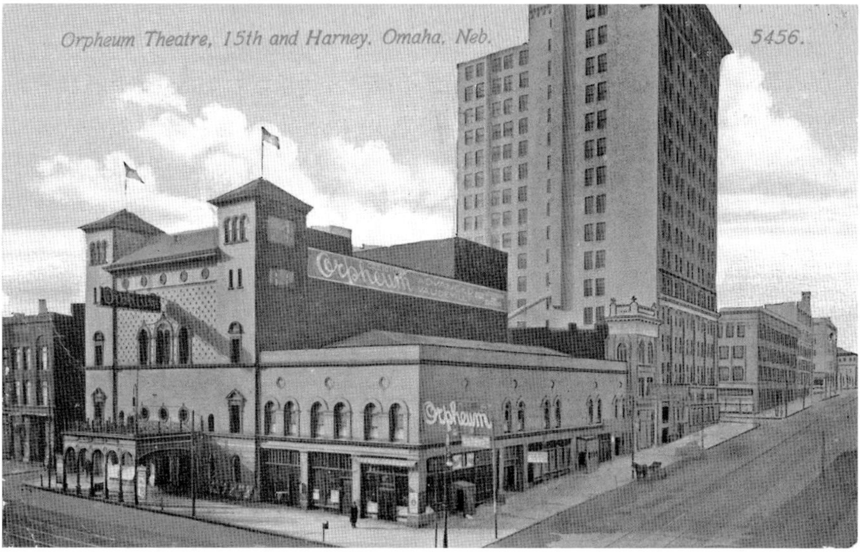

The Brandeis

210 South 16 Street

The Brandeis building, which has been converted to upscale apartments and condominiums, was once the city's most important department store, the heart of downtown's retail district. John Latenser Sr. designed the original Neo-Renaissance eight-story building that opened in 1906 and cost $1 million. Two floors were added in 1921. The building's exterior features lions above the seventh floor surrounding the entire building just below the original roof. Note architectural details such as the façade above the northeast corner's second floor. Older area residents remember such things as the store's elaborate Christmas window displays and its tearoom, which allowed turn-of-the-century women to lunch without escorts. The store, listed in the National Register of Historic Places, closed in 1980 as downtown declined as a retail center.[45]

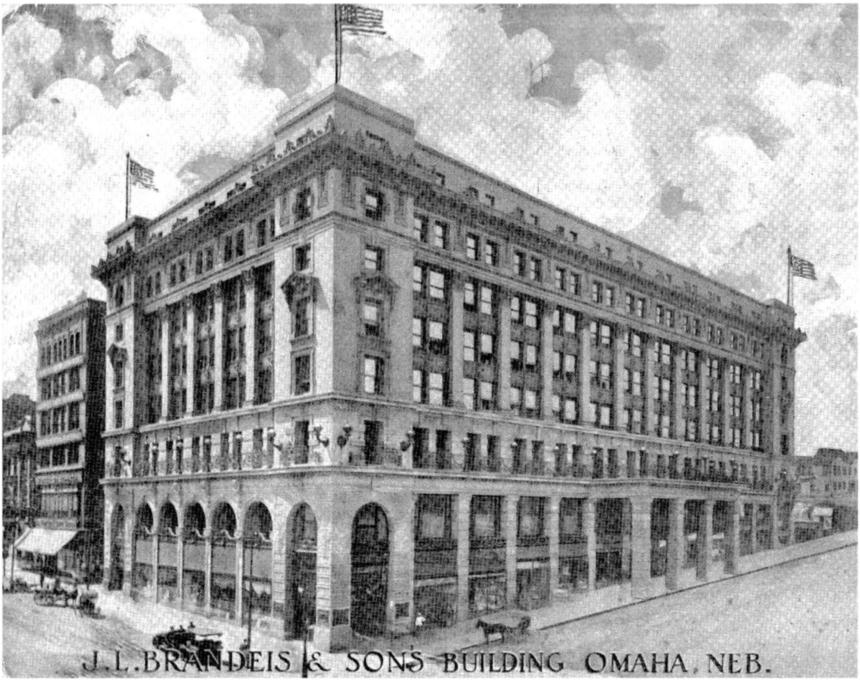

Above and opposite: Brandies Department Store was Omaha's leading retail operation for decades, featuring attractions like the Pompeian Room.

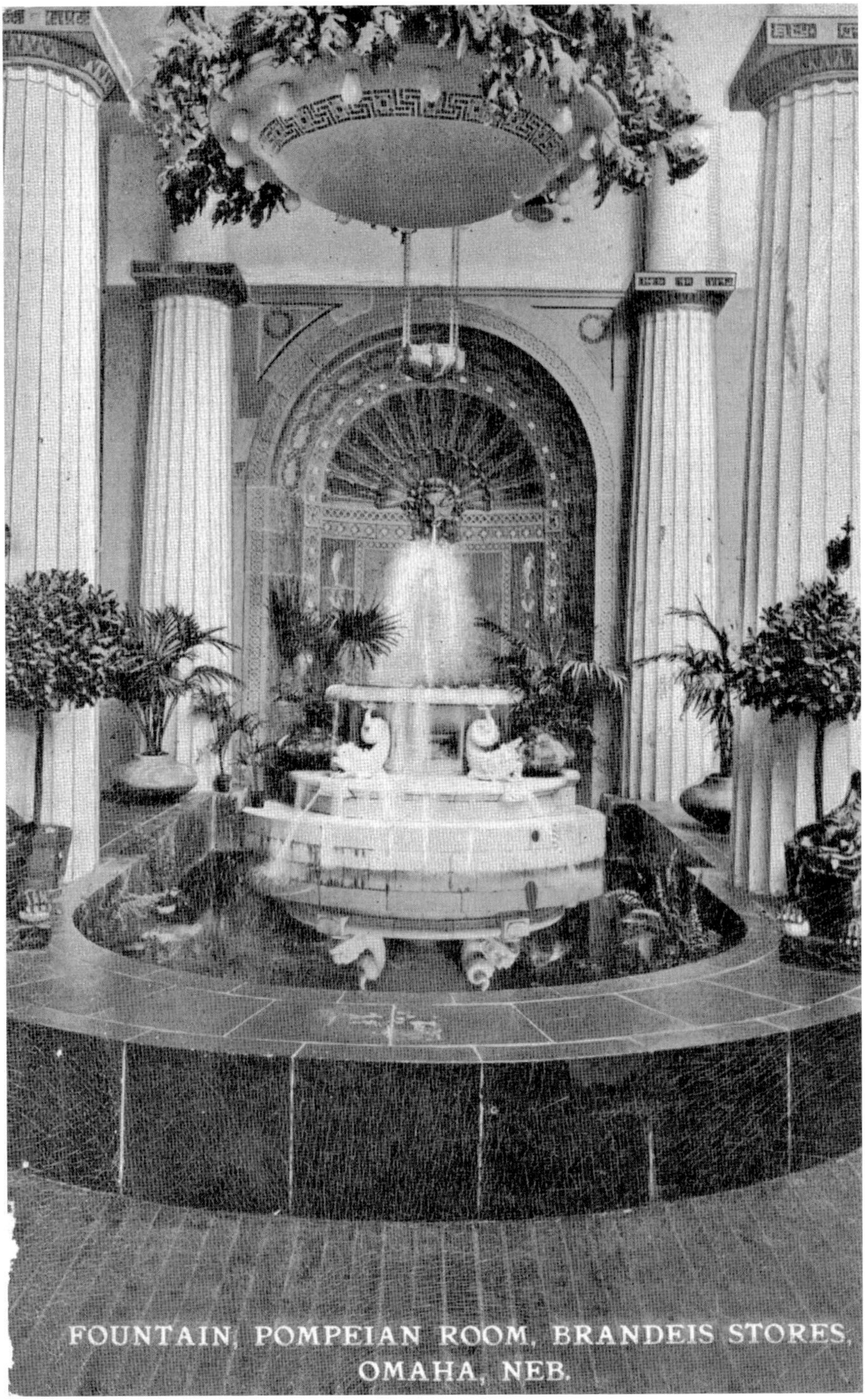
FOUNTAIN, POMPEIAN ROOM, BRANDEIS STORES,
OMAHA, NEB.

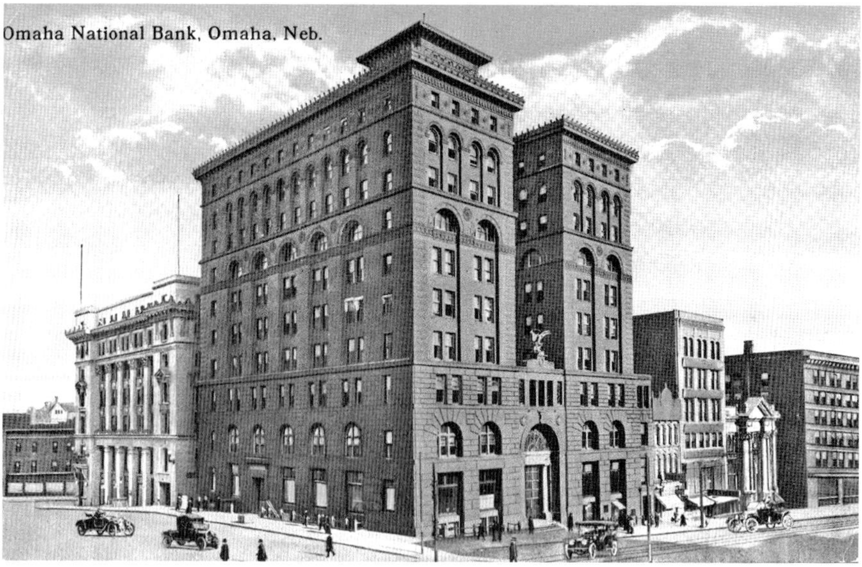

Old Omaha National Bank is now Kutak Law Firm headquarters.

The Omaha Building

1650 Farnam Street

This Italian Renaissance former bank building is home to Kutak Rock, Omaha's largest law firm, and houses the firm's extensive art collection. It was built in 1888–89 and was originally occupied by the New York Life Insurance before Omaha National Bank purchased it in 1909. Designed by Frederick Elmer Hill of the New York architectural firm of McKim, Mead and White, it was Omaha's first ten-story structure. In 1972, Omaha National Bank merged with another bank and moved out of the building. It was slated for demolition but was renovated in 1978 and is listed in the National Register of Historic Places.[46]

Douglas County Courthouse

1701 Farnam Street

The Douglas County Courthouse is a six-story Bedford stone French Renaissance Revival Building designed by Omaha architect John Latenser Sr. It opened in 1912 and is listed in the National Register of Historic Places. The building was almost destroyed in the infamous 1919 courthouse riot that resulted in the lynching of prisoner Will Brown, falsely accused of raping a white woman. Rioters also almost killed Omaha mayor Edward Smith, who was trying to stop the violence. The building houses local courts while county offices are located in the adjacent City-County Building. Visitors will note the interior's mosaic floors.[47]

Some of the other noteworthy buildings in the National Register of Historic Places downtown include:

- **Burlington Headquarters Building**, 1004 Farnam Street
- **City National Bank Building**, 16th and Harney Streets, connected to the Orpheum Theater
- **First National Bank Building**, 16th and Farnam Streets
- **Mary Rogers Kimball House**, 2236 St. Mary's Avenue
- **Nash Block**, 9th and Farnam Streets
- **Northern Natural Gas Building**, 2223 Dodge Street
- **Redick Tower**, 1504 Harney Street

Historic Parks

Downtown's two largest parks, Heartland of America Park and the Gene Leahy Mall, date to the late 1970s so are not profiled here but both were part of the major riverfront development program that began in the '70s. The Gene Leahy Mall is undergoing a complete renovation and is projected to reopen in 2021 as this book is going to print.

Lewis and Clark Landing/National Park Service Regional Headquarters

345 Riverfront Drive

This twenty-three-acre site on the riverfront is near the original site of the Lewis and Clark landing in 1804. It features a stairway to the river-level plaza. There are walking and bike trails that you can use to visit the National Park Service Regional Headquarters and **Bob Kerrey Pedestrian Bridge**. The bridge connects the landing to the **CHI Center**. The site includes the Lewis and Clark state historic marker, the Monument to Labor statue and Lewis and Clark interpretive exhibits.[48]

First National Spirit of Nebraska's Wilderness and Pioneer Courage Park

1400 Capitol Avenue/1601 Dodge Street

These collections of sculptures celebrating Nebraska's pioneers in covered wagons, buffalo and other reminders of the state's frontier era are at the locations indicated. The statues at 16th and Dodge are on the plaza in front of First National Bank's headquarters building, the tallest structure in downtown Omaha.

Freedom Park

2500 North 24th Street

This city park is a U.S. Naval Museum on the Missouri River and houses the USS *Marlin*, a submarine, and the USS *Hazard*, a World War II minesweeper. The *Hazard* first escorted ships sailing from San Francisco to Pearl Harbor and then worked with convoys to Eniwetok and Ulithi. In 1945, it was sent to Okinawa to perform anti-submarine patrols. A group of Omaha business leaders purchased it in 1971, and it is the only Admiral-class minesweeper left in the United States. The *Marlin* was launched in 1953 and decommissioned in 1973. It mostly performed target duty at the Fleet Sonar School in Key West.[49] The park is included here because it is historic but is not included on the tour route because it was closed to the public due to flood damage as this book was being researched.

THINGS TO DO

Search for the small restaurants, bars and coffee houses half-hidden among the major downtown buildings. Stop at important buildings like the courthouse or Omaha Building to enjoy their artistic and architectural treasures even if parking is a challenge. Joslyn Art Museum is free and offers free adjacent parking. Plan at least an hour or two there and enjoy lunch at its cafeteria, which features a Chihuly glass sculpture. Return to downtown for a live theatrical or musical performance offered at the Orpheum Theater or Holland Center in addition to all the major entertainment and sporting events at CHI Center and T.D. Ameritrade Park. As this goes to press, pandemic closures and restrictions were easing, but check websites for current information.

4
CREIGHTON, CATHEDRAL AND GOLD COAST

During the Gilded Age of the 1870s through 1890s, Omaha grew from a muddy village into a prosperous city with a sense of unlimited horizons. Its industries boomed, and immigrants poured in for jobs in railroading, meatpacking and manufacturing. Entrepreneurs made fortunes in banking, retail and other fields. They invested these fortunes in lavish homes overlooking downtown and in institutions and landmarks that remain iconic more than a century later.

To revisit Omaha during this period, tour the area that includes Creighton University, the Cathedral area and the Gold Coast/Blackstone district west of downtown. Drop by Creighton University, founded during this period, with its lovely St. John's Church. Savor the ambiance of streets lined with mansions designed by some of Omaha's top architects and tour Thomas Rogers Kimball's masterpiece, the majestic St. Cecilia's Cathedral. Stop at nearby Joslyn Castle, home of George and Sarah Joslyn. Drive through the Gold Coast's historic buildings south of Dodge Street and enjoy the entertainment options in the renovated Blackstone District.

This segment of Omaha demonstrates how preserving historic buildings can enliven and enhance life in a community more than a century later.

Windstorm Impacted Cathedral's History

Although Omaha's Easter tornado in 1913 ripped through the Cathedral neighborhood, a windstorm on November 21, 1917, did more damage to the actual construction site of the massive cathedral. *St. Cecilia's Cathedral*, a history of the cathedral published to celebrate its diamond jubilee in 1980, described what happened to the old St. Cecilia's Catholic Church that the cathedral replaced: "At the height of the storm, the wind toppled a scaffolding of 130 feet being used in erecting the new cathedral. The scaffolding fell squarely in the middle, on top of the wood structure of St. Cecilia's church standing next to the cathedral, leaving only the belfry in the front and the sacristy to in the rear untouched. The wooden church was literally cut in two. The debris did not harm the altar, nor did the sanctuary lamp cease to burn during the storm. The cross on top of the cupola also still stood."

The destruction of the old small church hastened plans to move into the cathedral although it was unfinished. Builders quickly put the cathedral into condition to hold services. The parish celebrated the first mass there on Sunday, November 25, 1917, coincidentally the feast of St. Cecilia. Meanwhile, construction continued for decades as funds were raised to pay for it. St. Cecilia's was finally consecrated in 1959.*

---

* Werthman, St. Cecilia's Cathedral, 128.

SUGGESTED ROUTE

This tour route includes navigation directions. The remainder of the chapter gives information on sites, organized by category. Within categories such as state historic markers or landmark buildings, sites are listed by their order in the tour.

1. **Creighton University**, 24th and California Streets
   Drive north on 24th Street past Creighton, Omaha's Jesuit university founded in 1878. Although the campus is not open to car traffic on either side of 24th, park on a nearby street if you want to walk along the campus mall to see St. John's Church

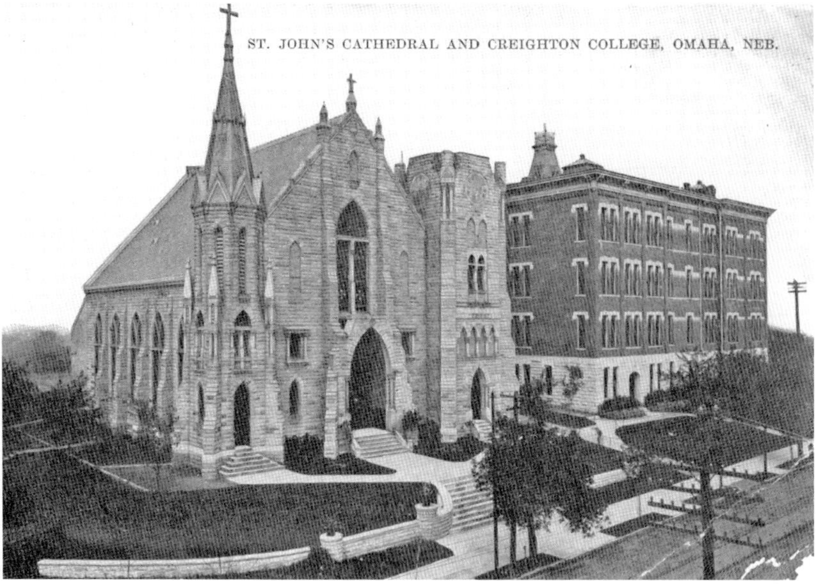

St. John's Church at Creighton University.

with its fountain in front. The Jesuit Gardens to the north of the church include a closed historic observatory.

2. **Bemis Park**, 33rd and Cuming Street. Take 24th to Cuming Street and go west past Bemis Park on the north side. Notice the Victorian mansions overlooking it. To visit the park, enter from 33rd Street.
3. **Walnut Hill Reservoir**, 38th Street and Lafayette Avenue. Continue west on Cuming to 38th Street and take it north to Lafayette Avenue to see the fountain in the Walnut Hill Reservoir.
4. **Duchesne Academy of the Sacred Heart**, 3601 Burt Street. Go north on 38th Street to Hamilton Street and then west to 40th. Take 40th to Cuming and go east on Cuming to 38th Street. Turn right at the light and go a block south to Burt Street. The Duchesne campus is on the right. Go east on Burt to 36th Street and then south past the campus to California Street. Take California to 40th Street.
5. **St. Cecilia's Cathedral**, 701 North 40th Street. Drive north on 40th Street to the Cathedral and park on the street or in the parking lot west of the cathedral. Tour architect Thomas Rogers Kimball's masterpiece.

6. **Mansions on 38th Street/Joslyn Castle**, 308 North 40th Street. Take 40th to Burt Street and then go east to 38th Street and drive south past several blocks of mansions. At Davenport Street, turn right and go about a block west to the entrance of Joslyn Castle's parking lot on the north. Park there to visit the estate of George and Sarah Joslyn and stroll through the lovely grounds.
7. **First Central Congregational Church**, 421 South 36th Street and **First Unitarian Church**, 3114 Harney Street. Return to 38th Street and go south to Harney Street, then go east past the back of the Kimpton Cottonwood Hotel (formerly the Blackstone Hotel), First Central Congregational Church, the south side of Mutual of Omaha and First Unitarian Church. Continue to 24th Street and go north to Farnam Street. Stay on Farnam to the end of the tour.
8. **Kountze Memorial Lutheran Church**, 201 South 27th Street. See the state historic marker at the first Lutheran church west of the Missouri River. Continue west on Farnam Street, noting the historic homes and buildings, Midtown Crossing and Mutual of Omaha.
9. **Gottlieb Storz House**, 3708 Farnam Street. This historic home of a local beer baron is on the north side of Farnam.
10. **Kimpton Cottonwood (Blackstone) Hotel/Blackstone Historic District**, 302 South 36th Street. Park on the street and walk along Farnam to about 40th Street past more historic homes and businesses (some restored). There are interesting buildings on Harney Street. Stop at one of the coffeehouses, bars or restaurants.

HISTORICAL MARKERS AND LANDMARKS

Nebraska Historical Markers

Before Creighton

1821 California Street (east end of the Creighton campus)

Between the 1730s and 1760s, what is now the eastern portion of Creighton University's campus housed an Oto Indian earth lodge village that extended to downtown. In 1804, Lewis and Clark recorded the ruins as an "ancient village .of the Otoes on mounds." Archaeological evidence shows periodic Native American residence in the general vicinity for some twelve thousand years.

This marker also celebrates Jesuit work with Native people beginning in the 1600s. In 1839, Jesuits, including Father Pierre DeSmet, a famed missionary and explorer, established a mission for the Potawatamie tribe across the Missouri River.[50] To see this marker, park somewhere on or near campus and walk down the mall east to 18th and California.

George and Sarah Joslyn Home

308 North 40th Street

The Joslyns made their fortune in the ready-print news business. They bought the Sutphen farm as the site for their home in 1893. Omaha architect John McDonald designed this thirty-four-room Scottish manor, completed in 1903, which is popularly called Joslyn Castle. The five-acre site includes a former carriage house, as well as landscaped grounds and parking.[51] Sarah Joslyn later developed and paid for Joslyn Art Museum as a memorial to her husband.

Joslyn Castle is open for tours on arrangement and is a popular venue for special events. Check the website for information.

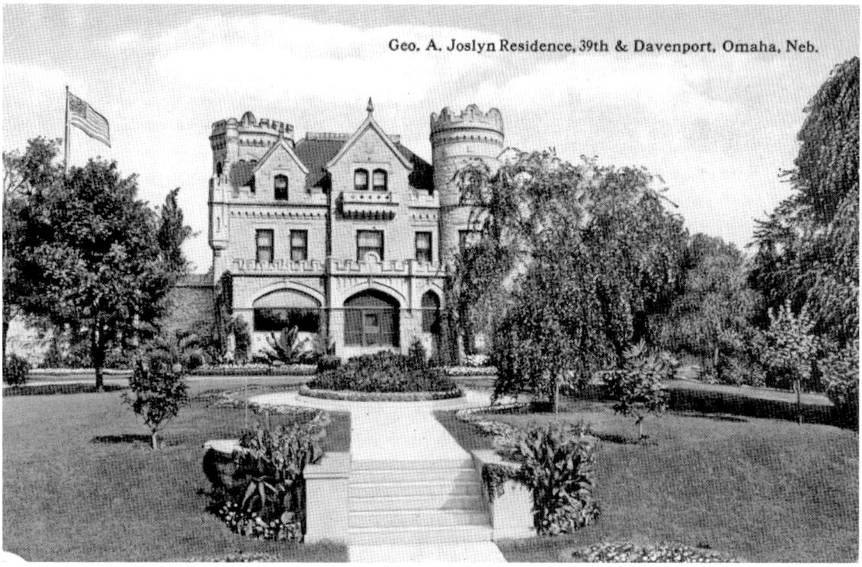

Joslyn Castle was home to arts patron Sarah Joslyn.

Kountze Memorial Lutheran Church

201 South 27th Street

Nebraska Territory's first Lutheran missionary, Reverend Henry Kuhns, and fourteen charter members organized Emanuel Evangelical Lutheran Church in 1858. The congregation opened a small church at 1210 Douglas Street in 1862 and completed a larger church at 16th and Harney in 1885, with a gift from charter member and banker Augustus Kountze. The congregation renamed the church in his father's honor. It completed this white limestone building in 1906 and later added the fellowship hall and educational wing. Kountze Memorial is the oldest continuous Lutheran congregation west of the Missouri River.[52]

Historic Districts

Gold Coast Historic District

36th, 40th, Jones and Cuming Streets

This thirty-block area includes most of the Cathedral and Blackstone areas and features the opulent homes where many city business and cultural leaders lived around the turn of the last century. The area was added to the National Register of Historic Places in 1997. Most of the historic homes listed later in the chapter are in the district.[53]

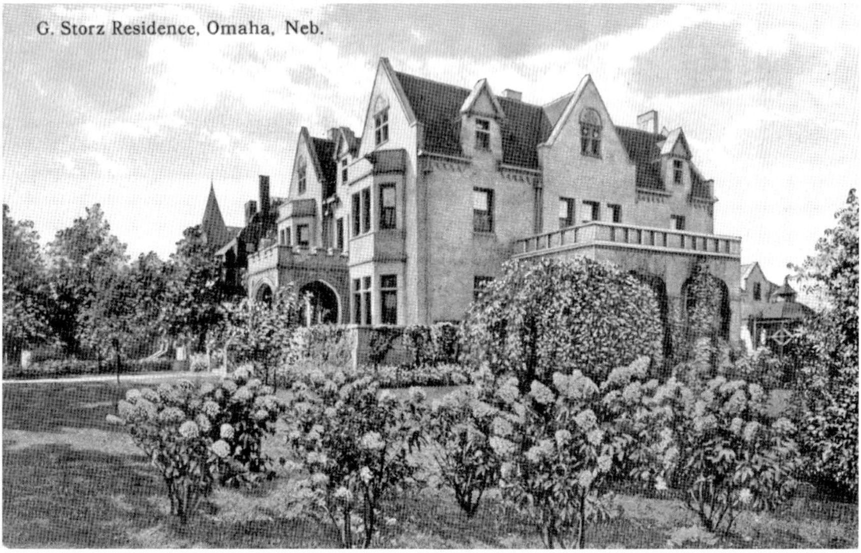

Gottlieb Storz House at 37th and Farnam Streets.

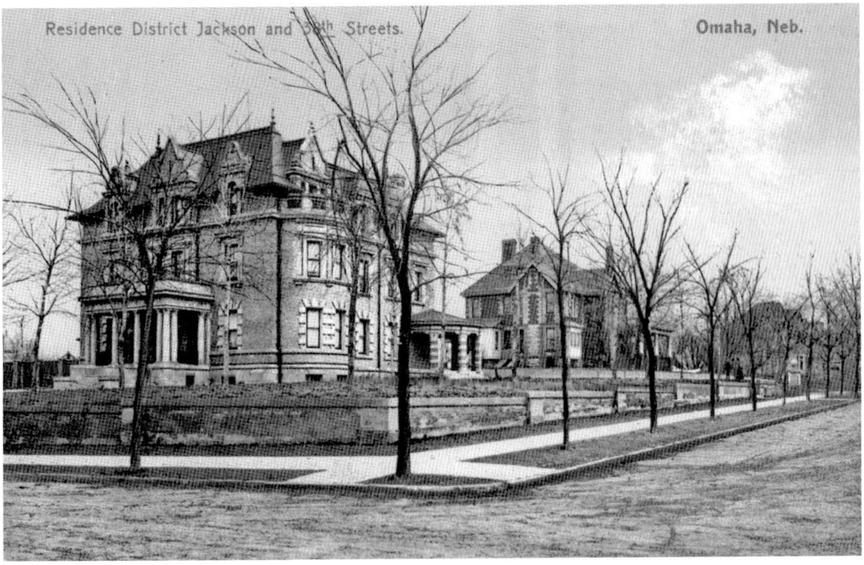

Gilded Age mansions in Gold Coast Historic District.

Historic Buildings

St. John's Catholic Church

Creighton University campus

St. John's Church, about half a block west of the 24th Street entrance to Creighton, was built in 1887–88 at the urging of Sarah Emily Creighton, a member of the university's founding family. This stone Gothic edifice features the sculptured stations of the cross that John Creighton donated in his wife, Sarah's, memory. The Jesuit Gardens north of Creighton Hall include an early observatory that is not open.

Duchesne Academy of the Sacred Heart

3601 Burt Street

This all-girls high school opened in 1881 as a boarding school that later accepted day students. It was run by the Religious of the Sacred Heart, a French order noted for providing an excellent liberal arts education. Between 1915 and 1968, Duchesne also operated a women's college.

Construction of this Omaha Landmark building began in 1882. It boasted steam heat, fireplaces, running water, telephones, bathrooms on every floor and an elevator. In 1910, Thomas Rogers Kimball designed a beautiful chapel on the original building's west side that included an altar he created with marble from Carrara, Italy. Kimball also designed occasional alterations on the school's campus.[54]

St. Cecilia's Cathedral

701 North 40th Street

When Omaha bishop Richard Scannell hired Thomas Rogers Kimball to design St. Cecilia's, one of the nation's ten largest cathedrals, they were making a statement that Omaha had become a city of permanence and culture. This magnificent church with its 222-foot towers on what was then the western end of Omaha became a source of pride for the entire city and was one of the first local buildings in the National Register of Historic Places.[55] It replaced the old St. Philomena's Cathedral at 9th and Howard Streets, which stood in the way of downtown's expanding warehouse district.[56]

Kimball, designer of many buildings at the 1898 Trans-Mississippi Exposition, created a Spanish Renaissance Revival church to honor the early Spanish explorers who had supposedly passed through Omaha. Ground was broken in 1905, and the church was used for decades before it was consecrated in 1959. Construction was on a pay-as-you-go basis.

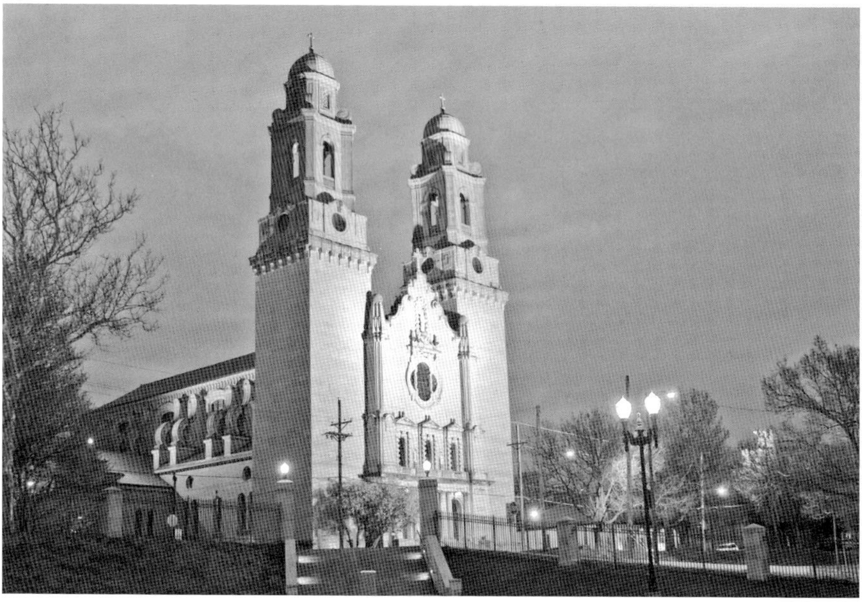

St. Cecilia's Cathedral lit up at night. *Photo by Carol Mccabe.*

All of the cathedral's art is original, and much of it honors saints and holy people of the Americas. The stained-glass windows in the Our Lady of Nebraska Chapel are from a fifteenth-century church in Pamplona, Spain.

Kimball designed features such as the pulpit with its mahogany statues of six doctors of the church and the high main altar. Noted sculptor Albin Polasek created the thirteen-foot bronze crucifix that hangs over it, as well as the bronze relief stations of the cross.

Two chapels are used for private prayer or small services. The Nash Chapel on the cathedral's south side honors Edward Nash, a community leader who helped finance the building of the cathedral. The crystal chandelier is from the Nash home. The Our Lady of Nebraska Chapel on the north side features a statue of the Virgin Mary holding ears of corn in honor of the state. Polasek created the plaster model for it.[57]

Brochures for self-guided tours are available in the church. Plan on half an hour or more and don't miss the art gallery behind the sanctuary. St. Cecilia's is open to the public during the day, and parking is available in lots on the south and west sides, although access was restricted during the coronavirus pandemic. The former Cathedral High School building on the east is a museum of Cathedral and Omaha Archdiocesan history. Check the St. Cecilia's Cathedral website for more information.

First Central Congregational Church

421 South 36th Street

First Central Congregational Church was founded in 1856, making it one of Omaha's oldest congregations. It had several locations before moving to this building in 1922.[58]

Kimpton Cottonwood (Blackstone) Hotel

302 South 36th Street

The Blackstone Hotel was built in 1915 and became nationally famous for inventing the Reuben sandwich. For years, it was Omaha's premier hotel and one of the finest in the Midwest. It is listed in the National Register of Historic Places. It closed as a hotel in 1976 and was renovated as an office building in 1984. In 2021 it reopened as a historically renovated luxury hotel called the Kimpton Cottonwood. Although the original name cannot be used for legal reasons, the surrounding neighborhood is known as the Blackstone District. Check the website for more information.

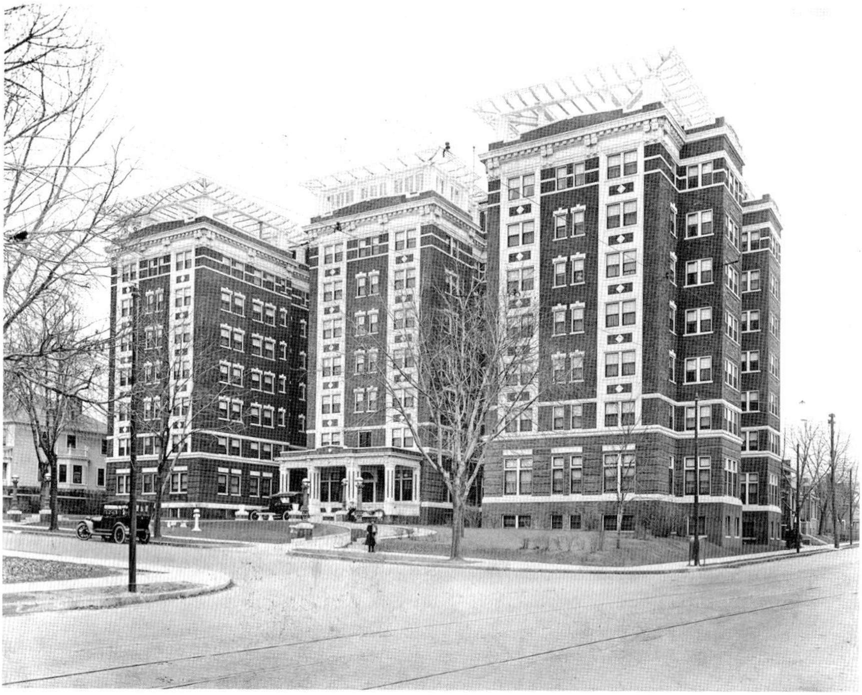

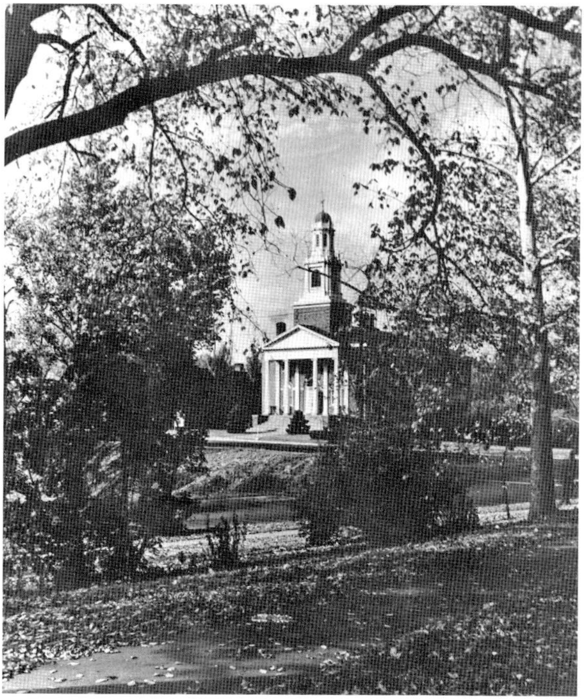

Above: Old Blackstone Hotel has been restored as the Kimpton Cottonwood Hotel.

Right: First Unitarian Church.

First Unitarian Church

3114 Harney Street

This Colonial Revival church designed by architects John and Alan McDonald is in the National Register of Historic Places. Former president William Howard Taft, who was president of the Unitarian Church Conference in the United States, presided over its 1917 cornerstone laying.[59]

Historic Houses

This area is home to the thirty-block Gold Coast Historic District listed in the National Register of Historic Places. It is roughly bounded by 36th, 40th, Jones and Cuming Streets. Within this district many individual homes also are listed in the National Register. Because most are private residences, they are not open to the public. One of the most famous is the Gottlieb Storz House.

Gottlieb Storz House

3708 Farnam Street

Omaha beer magnate Gottlieb Storz built this twenty-seven-room mansion, designed by Thomas Rogers Kimball, in 1905. In 1955, it was the site of the premiere party for the movie *Strategic Air Command* starring Jimmy Stewart and June Allyson. Both attended the party along with General Curtis LeMay, commander of the Air Force's Srategic Air Command. The mansion's top floor is the Adele and Fred Astaire Ballroom, which celebrates the legendary dancers' Omaha roots. The mansion is listed in the National Register of Historic Places and remains a private home.[60]

Other Historic Houses and Buildings

The following is a listing of area houses and other buildings in the National Register that can be seen from the street on a walking or driving tour. Some are outside the Gold Coast District. Check Wikipedia for information on individual homes.

- **Bradford-Pettis House**, 400 South 39th Street
- **Brandeis-Millard House**, 500 South 38th Street
- **Garneau-Kilpatrick House**, 3100 Chicago Street

- **Havens-Page House**, 101 North 39th Street
- **Charles D. McLaughlin House**, 507 South 38th Street
- **Dr. Samuel Mercer House**, 3920 Cuming Street
- **The Nottingham Apartments**, 3304 Burt Street
- **Porter-Thomsen House**, 3426 Lincoln Boulevard
- **Saunders School**, 415 North 41st Avenue
- **Selby Apartments**, 830 South 37th Street and 825 South 37th Avenue
- **Turner Court Apartments**, 3106 Dodge Street
- **Twin Towers**, 30th and Farnam/Douglas Streets
- **Edgar Zabriskie House**, 3524 Hawthorne Avenue

Historic Parks

Bemis Park

33rd and Cuming Streets

This park is part of the Bemis Park Landmark Heritage District between 33rd and Cuming Streets, Hawthorne Avenue and Glenwood Avenue. The area was developed between 1889 and 1922 and is noted for its Queen Anne, Arts and Crafts and Neo-Classical homes, many of which have been restored in the modern era. The park includes a playground and at one time featured a lagoon. It was designated an Omaha landmark in 1983.[61]

Walnut Hill Reservoir

38th and Lafayette

The Walnut Hill Reservoir was built as part of the original Omaha Water Works in 1882. Working with gravity, the reservoir drew water from the Missouri River near downtown, bringing it uphill to North 40th and Hamilton Streets. Within a decade of construction, that system was changed so that water was drawn from the Florence Water Works to Walnut Hill and distributed from there.[62]

THINGS TO DO

We suggest you end your tour in the Blackstone District because it is full of coffeehouses, bars and restaurants, most of them new and upscale. However, the total area also includes traditional neighborhood favorites like the Radial Café north of the Cathedral on 40th Street, which is noted for large servings

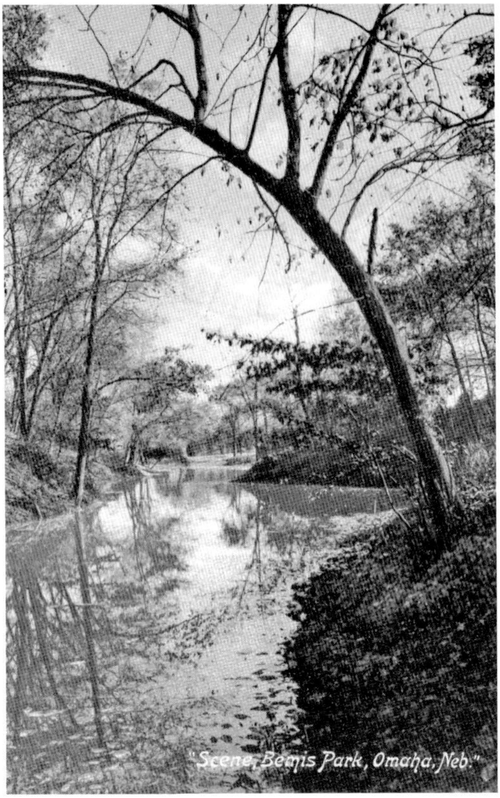

Right: Lagoon that formerly cut through Bemis Park.

Below: Walnut Hill Reservoir. *Photo by Carol Mccabe.*

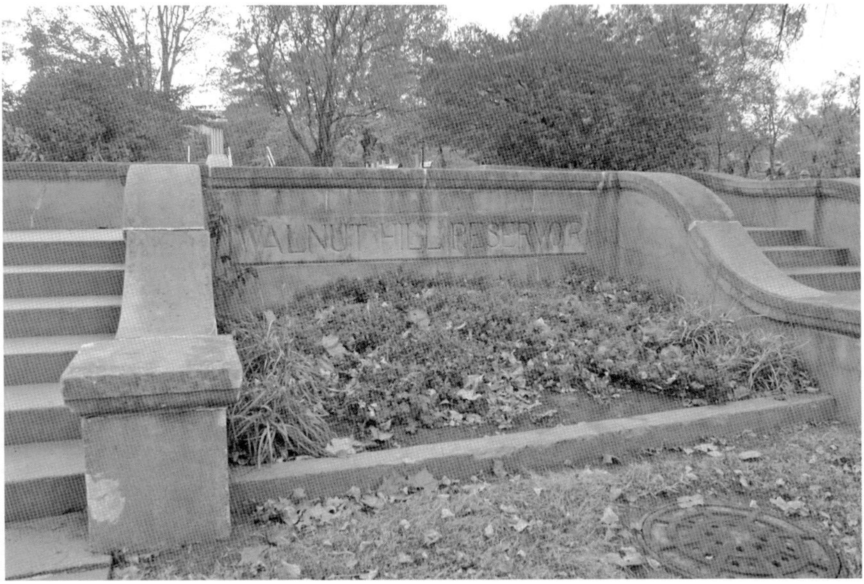

and modest prices. Numerous small ethnic restaurants and food stores line Saddle Creek Road about half a mile to the west. Some morning, as the sun is rising, walk along 38th Street past the mansions. The changing colors of the Cathedral may remind you of an impressionist painting, and it's easy to imagine rich Omahans traveling those streets in their carriages during the Gilded Age. Afterward, have breakfast at one of the small local cafés or coffee shops.

5

DUNDEE AND AKSARBEN

Pick a nice day for your excursion through midtown Omaha, since the best way to enjoy much of it is on foot. Stroll through the picturesque Dundee commercial area along Underwood Avenue between about 48th and 52nd Streets. Visit some of the boutiques, cafés and coffeehouses and note the historic streetlights and hanging flowerpots. There are good reasons why Dundee is considered one of Omaha's loveliest neighborhoods. Then head to Memorial and Elmwood Parks for more walking. Soak in the neighborhood ambiance.

Head south of Elmwood Park to the Aksarben area, where University of Nebraska at Omaha's Scott Campus and Aksarben Village occupy the site of the old racetrack and coliseum. As you wander through the shops, restaurants, bars and Stinson Park in this lively development, recall the crowds that once packed the track for Thoroughbred racing or filled the coliseum for concerts featuring major stars or participated in the old Ak-Sar-Ben Coronation balls that crowned the year's king and queen of the mythical kingdom of Quivera.

Tour attractions also include three historic cemeteries, the University of Nebraska at Omaha (UNO), historic churches and some of Omaha's storied residential areas. Take a break from museums to sample a section of Omaha where people lived the good life a century ago and have preserved that ambiance today.

Japanese Bombed Dundee Neighborhood

During the night of April 18, 1945, a blast jolted the Dundee neighborhood. Residents heard a loud boom and saw a flash of light. Word spread that an incendiary device that had floated from Japan by balloon had caused the explosion, one of a handful of such bombs that reached the United States. Fortunately, it caused no damage.

The government asked residents not to talk about the bomb to keep the Japanese from knowing how far inland it had come. People complied because, like most Americans at the time, they were highly patriotic. Residents collected tin cans for the war effort, and planted victory gardens in their spacious yards. When President Franklin Roosevelt had died just six days before the bomb exploded, they prayed for him at St. Margaret Mary Catholic Church and Dundee Presbyterian Church.

The people of Dundee were typical of all area residents. During World War II south of Omaha, workers at the Glenn Martin Bomber Plant built thousands of B-29s, including the *Enola Gay*, which carried the first atomic bomb to Hiroshima in August, helping end the war soon after.

But the bombing of Dundee has a special place in local home front lore. Today, there's a plaque on the southwest corner of 50th Street and Underwood Avenue commemorating the bomb that brought the war to Dundee's quiet streets.*

* Horan, "Bombs Bursting in Air."

SUGGESTED TOUR ROUTE

This tour route includes navigation directions. The remainder of the chapter gives information on sites, organized by category. Within categories such as state historic markers or landmark buildings, sites are listed by their order in the tour. The tour begins at Holy Sepulchre Cemetery at Saddle Creek Road and Leavenworth and is generally bounded by 50th, 72nd and Center Streets and Underwood Avenue.

1. **Holy Sepulchre Cemetery**, Saddle Creek Road and Leavenworth Street. Go west on Leavenworth to the entrance of the cemetery. Follow the main drive to the top of the hill to see the Creighton family monument. The graves of Creighton/Creighton Prep Jesuits in order of their deaths are across the road just south of the Creighton family graves. Return to Leavenworth, go west to 50th and turn right. Take 50th Street north, crossing Dodge Street.
2. **Dundee Theater**, 4952 Dodge Street. The renovated historic theater, now run by Film Streams, is on the northeast corner of 50th and Dodge, with a parking lot on the northeast side of the building. Continue north on 50th to Underwood.
3. **Dundee Commercial District**, Underwood Avenue from about 48th Street to Happy Hollow Boulevard. Turn left at the light and go west on Underwood through the business district, passing old brick buildings, many of them repurposed. **Dundee Presbyterian Church** is on the north side of 53rd and Underwood across the street from **Brownell Talbot School**. Note the **Omaha Street Railway** marker at Happy Hollow and Underwood.
4. **Memorial Park**, 6005 Underwood Avenue. At 60th Street, turn left into the park's circular drive, passing memorial statues and the rose garden. Park on the drive to stop at the large war memorial and then continue on the circular drive to exit the park and return to Underwood. Continue driving west.
5. **Fairacres Neighborhood**, Fairacres Road and Underwood. Turn left onto Fairacres Road and go south down the road past some of Omaha's stateliest homes. Turn around at any point within Fairacres to return to Underwood and turn left.
6. **Omaha Community Playhouse**, 6915 Cass Street. Underwood becomes Cass Street at 69th Street. Turn left onto 69th to stop at the Community Playhouse or continue driving west to 72nd Street past the **Omaha Conservatory of Music** (formerly **Temple Israel**) on the south and **First United Methodist Church** on the north.
7. **Crossroads Mall**, 72nd and Dodge Streets. Turn left onto 72nd Street and drive past what remains of Crossroads (with much of the mall being demolished in 2021 for conversion to mixed-use development) on the west. Turn left onto Dodge Street and

go east to Happy Hollow Boulevard, passing the **University of Nebraska at Omaha** on the south and **St. Margaret Mary Catholic Church** and **Memorial Park** on the north.

8. **Elmwood Park**, Happy Hollow Boulevard and Dodge Street. Turn right onto Happy Hollow and drive south to the traffic roundabout. Curve right to enter Elmwood Park. Follow the road through Elmwood past the historic park pavilion, playgrounds, ballfields and a fountain. Park in any of the lots and enjoy walking around Elmwood. The park bisects the Elmwood Park Golf Course. Exit Elmwood at the traffic light at Pacific Street and cross Pacific to enter UNO's Scott Campus.
9. **Ak-Sar-Ben Field and the U.S. Air Mail**, UNO Scott Campus, parking lot on South 67th Street and Omaha, Stinson Park at the northwest corner of 67th Street and West Center Road. Drive south on 67th Street to see these two state historic markers at locations indicated.
10. **West Lawn-Hillcrest Cemeteries**, 60–57th and Center Streets. Turn left onto Center and drive east to the entrance to these two historic cemeteries on the south side of Center. Follow the road south through the cemeteries and return to Center and drive east to 52nd Street.
11. **Bohemian National Cemetery**, 52nd and Center Streets. Enter the cemetery just east of the traffic light (across from Hy Vee) and drive through it. Return to Center Street to conclude the tour.

HISTORICAL MARKERS AND LANDMARKS

Nebraska Historical Markers

Ak-Sar-Ben Field and the U.S. Air Mail

UNO Scott Campus, parking lot on South 67th Street

Ak-Sar-Ben Field was used extensively during the early development of the U.S. Postal Air Mail Service, with the first such flight from Chicago on May 15, 1920. The Omaha–San Francisco leg of the transcontinental route opened in September. Although the first flights were in the daytime, pilot Jack Knight took the first night mail flight from North Platte to Chicago in 1921, landing at Ak-Sar-Ben en route. In 1924, day-night coast-to-coast airmail service began.[63]

Omaha, Stinson Park

Northwest corner of 67th Street and West Center Road

In 1935, Omaha won horse racing's Triple Crown, making him one of the sport's immortals. His sire, Gallant Fox, won the honor in 1930, making them the only father-son Triple Crown combination. Omaha, a chestnut colt, was born in Kentucky and ridden in his great races by William "Smokey" Saunders. He retired to stud after his fourth season. Breeders who wanted to improve Nebraska's Thoroughbred stock brought him to Omaha in 1950. He lived at the Grove Porter Farm near Nebraska City where he was a stud until his death on April 25, 1959. Ak-Sar-Ben invited him to be buried here in honor of his role in American racing. A bronze sculpture of Omaha marks the horse's grave.[64]

Historic Businesses, Buildings, Parks and Sites

Dundee Theater

4952 Dodge Street

This renovated theater now operated by Film Streams art cinema opened in 1925 playing silent movies. In 1929, it installed sound equipment and was renovated for the first time in 1938. Over the years, it became known for its midnight showings of classic and cult films such as *The Rocky Horror Picture Show*, keeping the Dundee alive while competition from multiplexes forced the closing of other small-screen movie houses. After the Dundee closed for renovation in 2013, the Sherwood Foundation acquired it and turned the theater over to Film Streams. The completely remodeled theater specializes in independent art films and documentaries. It includes a refreshment center and hosts social event.[65] Check the website for information on hours and film showings.

Dundee Commercial District

Underwood Avenue between 48th and 52nd Streets

Dundee was developed in 1880 as one of Omaha's first suburbs but was annexed in 1915.[66] It has long been associated with its most famous resident, billionaire Warren Buffett, whose family ran Buffett & Sons Grocers at 5015 Underwood Avenue for many years. Buffett, who worked there as a teenager, still lives in the area south of Dodge Street and was married at Dundee Presbyterian Church. He has occasionally been spotted with other celebrities, such as Bono, at the eCreamery Ice Cream and Gelato shop just east of his family's old grocery store site now occupied by Dundee Bank.

Many of the businesses in today's downtown Dundee occupy renovated spaces that once housed longtime local establishments. eCreamery, at 50th and Underwood, for example, was a drugstore, and the CHI Health Clinic across the street was formerly a Hinky Dinky supermarket. The site of today's Avoli Osteria restaurant was Trovato's Italian Restaurant for fifty-two years. Trace the roots of various establishments as you wander the area.

Dundee Presbyterian Church
5312 Underwood Avenue
This church on the west edge of the Dundee business district was organized in 1901 and built this impressive edifice in 1928. Warren Buffett is one of many prominent Omahans associated with this congregation.[67]

Brownell-Talbot School
400 Happy Hollow Boulevard
The campus of this prestigious private school has been a neighborhood landmark since it moved to the area in the 1920s. Brownell Hall was organized as an Episcopal girls' boarding school and held Nebraska's first high school commencement ceremony in 1868. Today, Brownell-Talbot is coed and offers classes from pre-kindergarten through high school. The campus occupies part of the old Dundee Golf Course.

Fairacres Neighborhood Historic District
Fairacres Road
This iconic neighborhood between Underwood and Dodge was added to the National Register of Historic Places in 2017. It was originally platted in 1907 by the Dundee Realty Company and is noted for its gracious, large homes designed in revivalist styles, such as Tudor Revival. The Fairacres Road street is still paved with the original bricks. In 1941, the city annexed the district.[68] Residents have always included some of Omaha's most prominent families. The old Catholic archbishop's residence, now a private home, is located at the Dodge Street entrance to Fairacres.

Omaha Community Playhouse
6915 Cass Street
This nationally recognized community theater was founded in 1924 and is noted for giving legendary actors such as Henry Fonda, Marlon Brando and Dorothy McGuire their start in theater. The theater was located in a building constructed on Sarah Joslyn's pasture at 40th and Davenport for years but moved to this location in 1959. It has expanded several times. When Fonda

died, his memorials were directed to the playhouse. Check the website for information about hours when the lobby is open as well as information on current productions. The building features photos of past playhouse productions.

Crossroads Mall

72nd and Dodge Streets

This formerly major shopping mall was opened in 1960 as one of Omaha's first major malls. It has undergone several previous reconstructions, and in 2021 much of the old mall was demolished. As of this writing, the site is being completely reconfigured as a mixed-use retail development. The intersection of 72nd and Dodge has long been one of the busiest in Omaha and is the site of political protests as well as spontaneous public celebrations such as one that broke out when Nebraska won a national football championship.

University of Nebraska at Omaha

60th and Dodge Streets

The UNO campus on the south side of Dodge Street began as a private college and Presbyterian seminary. It was founded in 1908 as part of an effort to bring the old Bellevue College to Omaha, changing its name to the University of Omaha. The city took it over in 1930 and ran it as a municipal university until it joined the University of Nebraska in 1968.[69] Since then, the campus has greatly expanded with the construction of numerous buildings on the traditional campus in addition to expanding south across Pacific Street with a major presence in the Aksarben Village area.

St. Margaret Mary Church

61st and Dodge Streets

This church on the north side of Dodge Street across from UNO was built in 1951. The parish was organized in 1919 in a facility at 5002 California Street, which has been converted to apartments.[70]

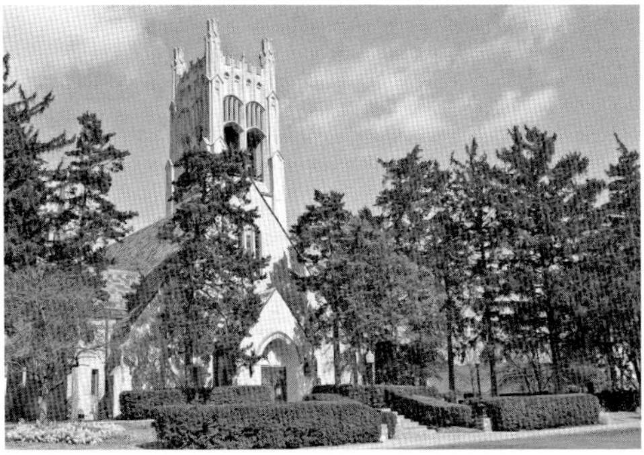

St. Margaret Mary Catholic Church. *Photo by Carol Mccabe.*

Historic Parks

Memorial Park

60th Street and Underwood Avenue
This inspiring park makes a powerful statement about patriotism and loss with its sweeping unobstructed uphill view north from Dodge Street to a stately colonnade. President Harry Truman dedicated the park, which was created in 1948 on the site of the old Happy Hollow Club and Dundee Golf Course as a memorial to area residents killed during World War II. Now it also honors the dead of subsequent wars. Omahans use the park for walking, running, sledding and other activities such major outdoor concerts, but there are no recreational facilities.[71]

The old **Dundee Golf Course** opened in about 1895. The first hole in this nine-hole course ran along what is now Happy Hollow Boulevard and the final hole was along Cass Street. There was a separate, shorter nine-hole course to the west for women. Both courses closed when the Omaha Country Club opened in 1899 in the Country Club Historic District north of Dundee. However, Happy Hollow Club opened an eighteen-hole course when it opened in 1907. That course covered parts of Memorial Park and the current Brownell Talbot campus.[72]

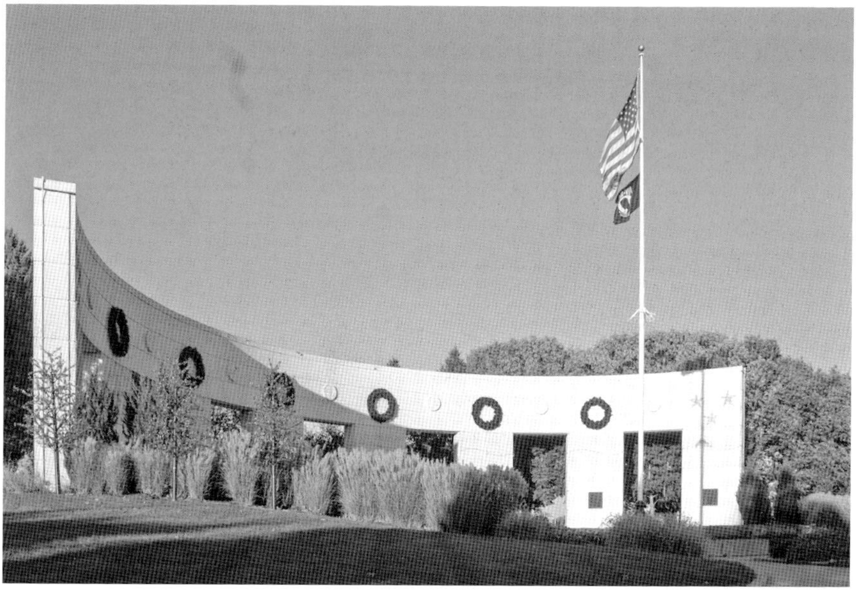

This page and opposite: War Memorial is the focus of Memorial Park. *Photo by Carol Mccabe.*

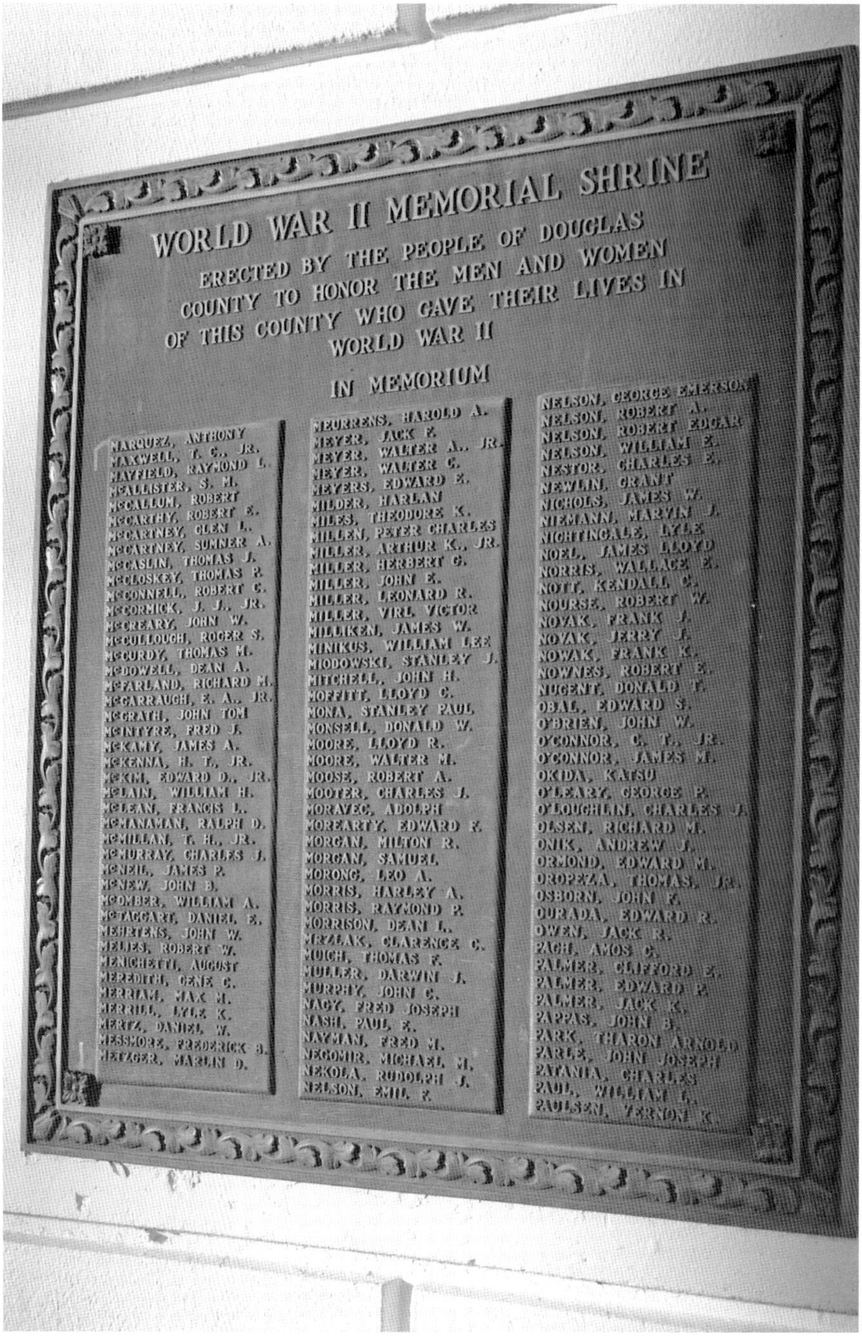
WORLD WAR II MEMORIAL SHRINE
ERECTED BY THE PEOPLE OF DOUGLAS
COUNTY TO HONOR THE MEN AND WOMEN
OF THIS COUNTY WHO GAVE THEIR LIVES IN
WORLD WAR II
IN MEMORIUM
MARQUEZ, ANTHONY
MAXWELL, T. C., JR.
MAYFIELD, RAYMOND L.
McALLISTER, S. M.
McCALLUM, ROBERT
McCARTHY, ROBERT E.
McCARTNEY, GLEN L.
McCARTNEY, SUMNER A.
McCASLIN, THOMAS J.
McCLOSKEY, THOMAS P.
McCONNELL, ROBERT C.
McCORMICK, J. J., JR.
McCREARY, JOHN W.
McCULLOUGH, ROGER S.
McCURDY, THOMAS M.
McDOWELL, DEAN A.
McFARLAND, RICHARD M.
McGARRAUGH, E. A., JR.
McGRATH, JOHN TOM
McINTYRE, FRED J.
McKAMY, JAMES A.
McKENNA, H. T., JR.
McKIM, EDWARD D., JR.
McLAIN, WILLIAM H.
McLEAN, FRANCIS L.
McMANAMAN, RALPH D.
McMILLAN, T. H., JR.
McMURRAY, CHARLES J.
McNEIL, JAMES P.
McNEW, JOHN B.
McOMBER, WILLIAM A.
McTAGGART, DANIEL E.
MEHRTENS, JOHN W.
MELIES, ROBERT W.
MENICHETTI, AUGUST
MEREDITH, GENE C.
MERRIAM, MAX M.
MERRILL, LYLE K.
MERTZ, DANIEL W.
MESSMORE, FREDERICK B.
METZGER, MARLIN D.
MEURRENS, HAROLD A.
MEYER, JACK F.
MEYER, WALTER A., JR.
MEYER, WALTER C.
MEYERS, EDWARD E.
MILDER, HARLAN
MILES, THEODORE K.
MILLEN, PETER CHARLES
MILLER, ARTHUR K., JR.
MILLER, HERBERT G.
MILLER, JOHN E.
MILLER, LEONARD R.
MILLER, VIRL VICTOR
MILLIKEN, JAMES W.
MINIKUS, WILLIAM LEE
MIODOWSKI, STANLEY J.
MITCHELL, JOHN H.
MOFFITT, LLOYD C.
MONA, STANLEY PAUL
MONSELL, DONALD W.
MOORE, LLOYD R.
MOORE, WALTER M.
MOOSE, ROBERT A.
MOOTER, CHARLES J.
MORAVEC, ADOLPH
MOREARTY, EDWARD F.
MORGAN, MILTON R.
MORGAN, SAMUEL
MORONG, LEO A.
MORRIS, HARLEY A.
MORRIS, RAYMOND P.
MORRISON, DEAN L.
MRZLAK, CLARENCE C.
MUICH, THOMAS F.
MULLER, DARWIN J.
MURPHY, JOHN C.
NAGY, FRED JOSEPH
NASH, PAUL E.
NAYMAN, FRED M.
NEGOMIR, MICHAEL M.
NEKOLA, RUDOLPH J.
NELSON, EMIL F.
NELSON, GEORGE EMERSON
NELSON, ROBERT A.
NELSON, ROBERT EDGAR
NELSON, WILLIAM E.
NESTOR, CHARLES E.
NEWLIN, GRANT
NICHOLS, JAMES W.
NIEMANN, MARVIN J.
NIGHTINGALE, LYLE
NOEL, JAMES LLOYD
NORRIS, WALLACE E.
NOTT, KENDALL C.
NOURSE, ROBERT W.
NOVAK, FRANK J.
NOVAK, JERRY J.
NOWAK, FRANK K.
NOWNES, ROBERT E.
NUGENT, DONALD T.
OBAL, EDWARD S.
O'BRIEN, JOHN W.
O'CONNOR, C. T., JR.
O'CONNOR, JAMES M.
OKIDA, KATSU
O'LEARY, GEORGE P.
O'LOUGHLIN, CHARLES J.
OLSEN, RICHARD M.
ONIK, ANDREW J.
ORMOND, EDWARD M.
OROPEZA, THOMAS, JR.
OSBORN, JOHN F.
OURADA, EDWARD R.
OWEN, JACK R.
PACH, AMOS C.
PALMER, CLIFFORD E.
PALMER, EDWARD P.
PALMER, JACK K.
PAPPAS, JOHN B.
PARK, THARON ARNOLD
PARLE, JOHN JOSEPH
PATANIA, CHARLES
PAUL, WILLIAM L.
PAULSEN, VERNON K.

Elmwood Park

Happy Hollow Boulevard and Dodge Street

This popular park dating to 1889 is a major midtown attraction with its playground, picnic areas, swimming pool, baseball and soccer fields and golf course. Its "Moorish Castle" pavilion was fifty years old when the federal Works Progress Administration restored it in 1939. During the 1930s, Elmwood featured a small man-made island in a lagoon that housed monkeys, but the monkeys escaped, causing problems. They were removed and their island converted into a concert space stage. The dense Elmwood Park ravine on the east side of the park with the creek running through it creates a pocket of wilderness in the middle of the city.[73]

Peony Park

78th and Cass Streets

Peony Park is not on the tour route because its site is now a Hy Vee grocery store. However, the park's history is worth noting. Peony Park was one of Omaha's top entertainment venues for years and began as a refreshment stand catering to automobile traffic in 1916. The Malec brothers, who owned the ten-acre site, replaced that stand with a gas station in 1919 and then added the Peony Inn restaurant in 1921. Eventually, they added a swimming pool, an amusement park and the Royal Grove ballroom after expanding the site to forty acres. The park was named after the peony farm across the road. The ballroom later hosted events such as the annual Omaha Press Club balls. During the civil rights era, the segregated pool was the site of protests and court battles that eventually integrated it. Despite efforts to upgrade the park by adding such things as a roller coaster, it could not remain competitive, went bankrupt and closed in 1994.[74]

Aksarben Village

Aksarben Village, which opened its first businesses in 2008, occupies an important historic location and is included on this tour because of this. The current spelling omits the traditional hyphens.

The Ak-Sar-Ben complex at 63rd and Shirley Streets included the racetrack, grandstands and Ak-Sar-Ben Coliseum, where concerts featuring major stars, rodeos and coronations were held. The complex was on the former grounds of the Nebraska State Fair and Omaha's first airport. The site included the remains of a one-mile racetrack built in 1898 that had not been used in years. When the new racetrack and grandstand opened in 1920, they replaced a racing facility in Benson that had closed.[75]

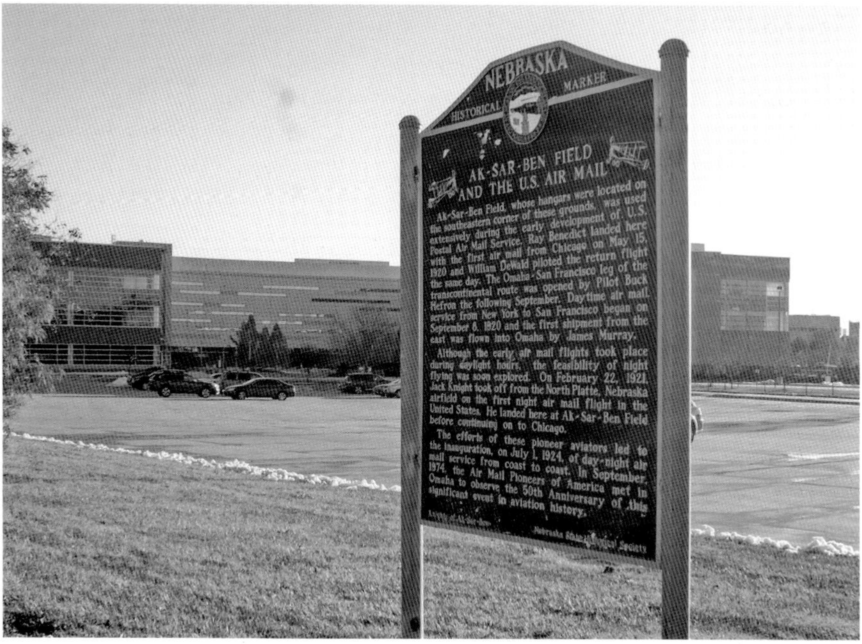

Historic marker of Ak-Sar-Ben Field. *Photo by Carol Mccabe.*

Ak-Sar-Ben, Nebraska spelled backward, was founded in 1895 to help Omaha recover from the depression of the 1890s by creating a major city festival. The group played a key role in organizing the Trans-Mississippi Exposition in 1898, and for years, its board of governors, the city's top business leaders, played a major role in civic endeavors of many types.

In 1924, Ak-Sar-Ben notified officials that it wished to build an exposition building and end its role in airmail service, which began in 1921. About the same time, the post office decided the field was too small, so airmail flights and the complex's role in aviation history ended that year.[76] With the 1920 opening of the horse racetrack and grandstand, Ak-Sar-Ben became increasingly identified with the races that drew thousands of spectators every spring until Nebraska banned horse racing in 1928. However, after racing resumed in 1935, the sport was a major public attraction for years until attendance declined due to competition from greyhound dog racing in Council Bluffs. In 1996, the county entity that had taken over the property ended horse racing.[77]

The Ak-Sar-Ben Coliseum, built in 1928, was home to the annual coronation of a major business leader as king and the daughter of a prominent family as queen of the mythical kingdom of Quivera. It also hosted the annual rodeo and livestock show, ice hockey and concerts featuring top entertainers that families could attend by paying a small fee to join the organization. The coliseum closed in 2002 and was torn down in 2005. Part of the property became the University of Nebraska at Omaha's Scott campus, and First Data Resources built a major complex on some of the land.[78]

Historic Cemeteries

Holy Sepulchre Cemetery

50th and Leavenworth Streets

This cemetery dates to 1873 and is the burial place for members of the Creighton family, including Edward and Mary Lucretia and John and Sarah Emily, founders of Creighton University. An obelisk commemorating the Creightons rises at the top of the cemetery's highest hill. Just south of the Creighton monument is the Priests Circle, where members of Creighton's Jesuit community are buried in the order of their deaths. Small, uniform plaques in the ground mark each grave.

Hillcrest Memorial Park Cemetery

60th and Oak Streets

Hillcrest Memorial Park Cemetery is just south of West Lawn Cemetery with graves marked only with tablets of bronze or granite. It is noted for its Singing Tower, a fifty-foot-high gothic sandstone shaft that rises from the crest of a hill that is one of the highest points in Douglas County. The tower, built in 1932, is a modified replica of the Edward Bok Memorial Tower in Florida. The tower, which got its name from the concerts that were broadcast from it, is octagonal and has three floors.[79]

West Lawn Cemetery

57th and Center Streets

West Lawn Cemetery was founded in 1910 and includes the West Lawn Mausoleum designed by Henry Bacon, who also designed the Lincoln Memorial in Washington, D.C. This marble structure featuring stained-glass windows and bronze doors was built in 1913–16 and contains hundreds of crypts and urns for ashes. It was Nebraska's first community mausoleum.[80]

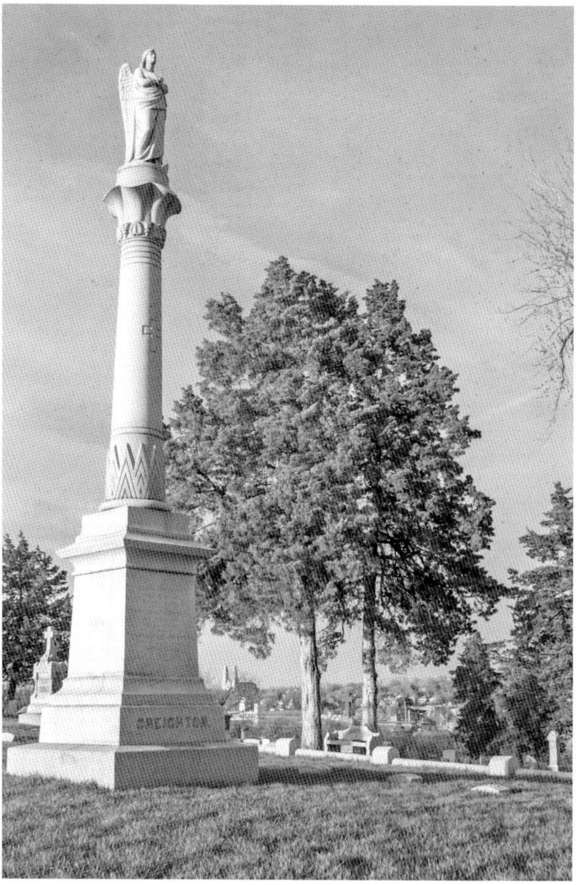

Left: Creighton family monument at Holy Sepulchre Cemetery. *Photo by Carol McCabe.*

Below: West Lawn Cemetery Mausoleum. *Photo by Carol McCabe.*

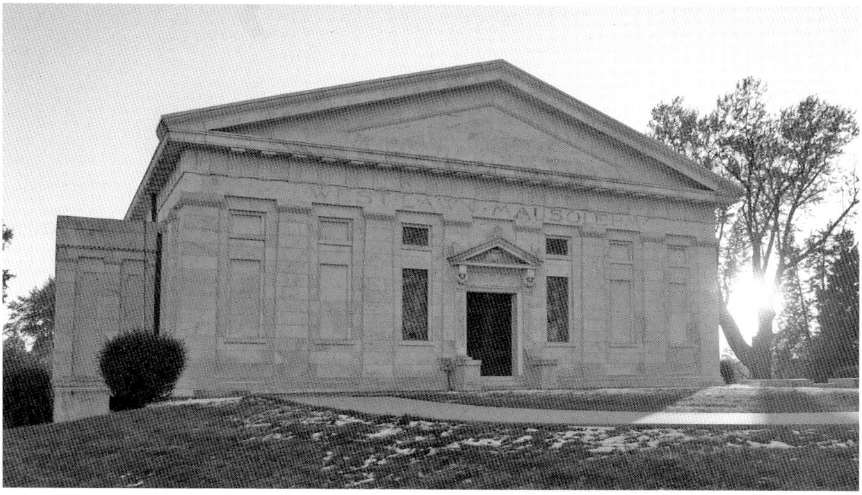

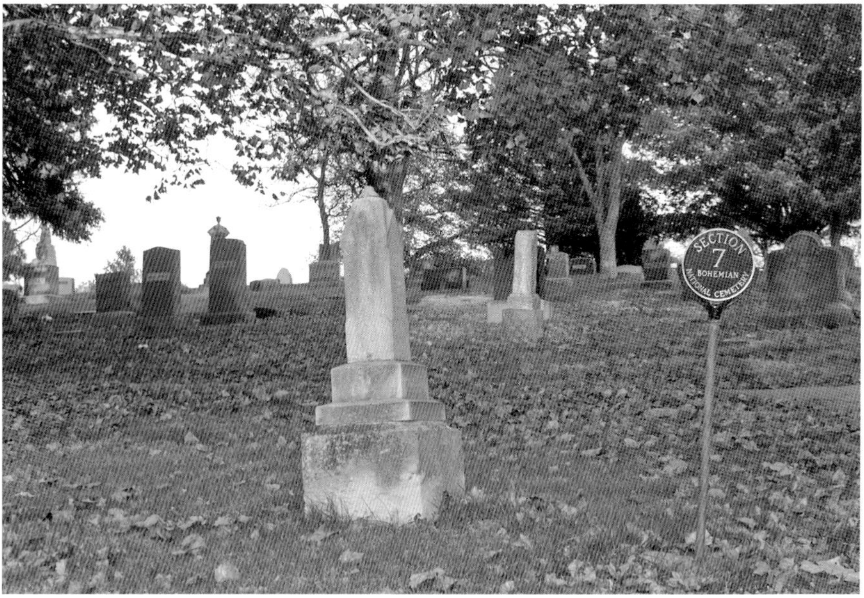

Marker in Bohemian National Cemetery. *Photo by Carol Mccabe.*

Bohemian National Cemetery

52nd and Center Streets

This cemetery in which only Bohemians are buried is adjacent to West Lawn Cemetery on the east. It was incorporated in 1883 and contains a monument that members of the Western Bohemian Fraternal Association dedicated to South Omaha journalist John Rosicky.[81]

THINGS TO DO

Take your pick of the many midtown entertainment and eating options. Choose from movie theaters, numerous bars, ethnic and gourmet restaurants, coffeehouses, pizza places and sweetshops. Trails in and near the parks are great for walking or biking. Whether you want to eat, shop or exercise, there's something for you.

6
NEAR SOUTH OMAHA

The area stretching from the Riverfront just south of downtown to I-80 and west to about 42nd Street includes the city's four top tourist attractions: Henry Doorly Zoo & Aquarium, the Old Market, the Durham Museum and Lauritzen Gardens, home of Kenefick Park's two historic Union Pacific locomotives.

There also are picturesque neighborhoods that were once ethnic enclaves, such as Little Italy and early suburbs like Hanscom Park, ethnic churches and numerous unique stores, restaurants, coffeehouses and bars in the Little Bohemia Historic District.

The magnificent Art Deco Union Pacific Depot, which is now Durham Museum, and the old Burlington Station, now KETV, as well as UP's Harriman Dispatch Center speak to Omaha's railroad heritage.

Hint: Touring the zoo takes about half a day of strenuous walking, so consider two or more trips to see everything, beginning or ending one day by eating at the Old Market. Then spend an hour or two strolling through the market, stopping in shops and art galleries/exhibits.

SUGGESTED TOUR ROUTE

This eight-mile tour route includes navigation directions. The remainder of the chapter gives information on sites, organized by category. Within categories such as state historic markers or landmark buildings, sites are

Gangland Violence Strikes Little Italy

Throughout Prohibition, Omahans continued to drink, and bootleggers from the Little Italy area south of downtown were delighted to accommodate them. Prohibition was sometimes called the "noble experiment," but it increased crime locally and nationally. The respectable Omahans who patronized the bootleggers and socialized at their speakeasies were among the new lawbreakers, at least technically. Some of Little Italy's old buildings still have tunnels and underground rooms dating to the era.

Prohibition ended nationally in 1932 and in 1934 in Nebraska. In Omaha, the former bootleggers who were planning to open legal bars and restaurants included Giuseppina Marcuzzo. But her neighbors were nervous about her preparations to open the Italian Gardens Restaurant at 1228 South 6th Street. Many of them signed a petition to delay the restaurant's opening—with good reason. Omaha was experiencing a series of gangland bombings connected with racketeering, and neighbors feared violence in their area.

On October 10, 1934, a day before the planned opening, a bomb exploded inside the restaurant, extensively damaging the building and shattering the windows of nearby buildings. Marcuzzo rushed to the site and fainted but was determined to rebuild. Police investigated but never charged anyone with the crime. They blamed the incident on racketeering feuding.

Marcuzzo repaired the damage and opened the Italian Gardens. It became highly successful, one of many fine Italian restaurants that made Little Italy a center of local night life. Eventually, Marcuzzo passed the restaurant on to her sons, and it remained in the family until the 1960s. It has since closed.*

* Reiner, Kim, *Lost Restaurants of Omaha*, 71–73.

listed by their order in the tour. Tour directions mention some of the major buildings you will pass, but numerous others line the streets.

1. **Field Club**, 36th Street and Woolworth Avenue. Begin tour at the Field Club at 36th and Woolworth. Go east on Woolworth through the historic neighborhood.
2. **Gerald Ford Birth Site**, 3202 Woolworth Avenue. The Gerald Ford Birth Site is on the north side of 32nd Avenue and Woolworth.
3. **Hanscom Park**, 1899 South 32nd Avenue. Turn right onto 32nd Avenue at Woolworth and follow it several blocks to the park's entrance on the left. Take the main road north through the park past the greenhouses. At the stop sign, veer south to see the lagoon on the left. Exit the park at Martha Street, turn left onto it and drive east for several miles.
4. **Lauritzen Gardens/Kenefick Park**, 100 Bancroft Street. Take Martha to 10th Street, passing through several historic ethnic neighborhoods. **Assumption Ukrainian Catholic Church** (formerly St. John's Greek Orthodox Church) is on the south at 16th Street, and **Sokol Auditorium** on the north at 13th Street. The **Little Bohemia Historic District** is north on 13th Street. Martha dead ends at 10th Street at the site of the old **Creighton Memorial St. Joseph's Hospital**. A few remnants of the hospital campus, once the largest in Nebraska, are still visible. Turn south onto 10th Street and go to Bancroft Street. Head east on Bancroft into Lauritzen Gardens. Kenefick Park, in the gardens, is only accessible on foot, but the locomotives are visible from Interstate 80. Return on Bancroft to 10th Street and turn left.
5. **Omaha's Henry Doorly Zoo & Aquarium**, 3701 South 10th Street. Follow 10th Street south to the entrance to the zoo on the left or park in a parking lot on the right. Note the large zoo billboard on the hill that was formerly Rosenblatt Stadium's scoreboard. The **Infield at the Zoo** preserves College World Series history on the site of the old stadium, which is now part of the zoo. Follow the exit signs from the zoo to 13th Street, turn right and take 13th Street through the Little Bohemia Historic District to Pacific Street.

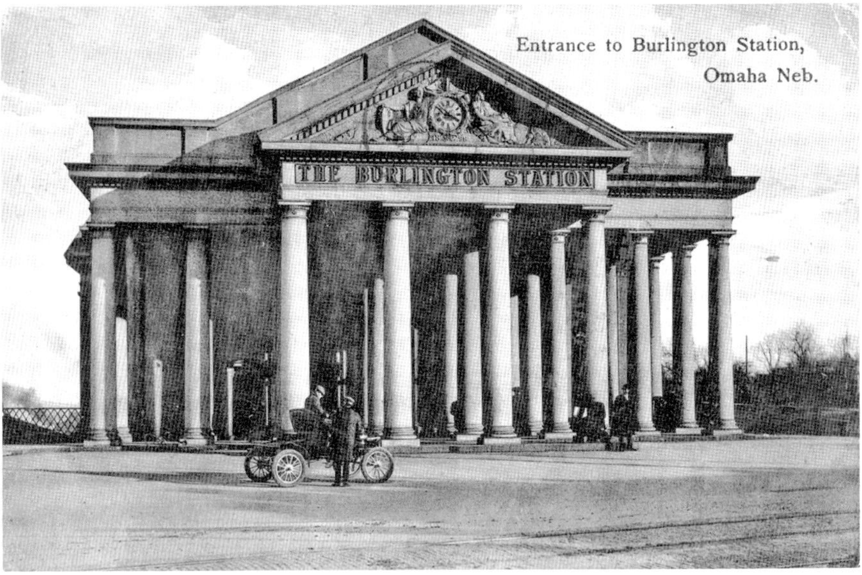

Columns of demolished Burlington Station were moved to the University of Nebraska–Lincoln campus.

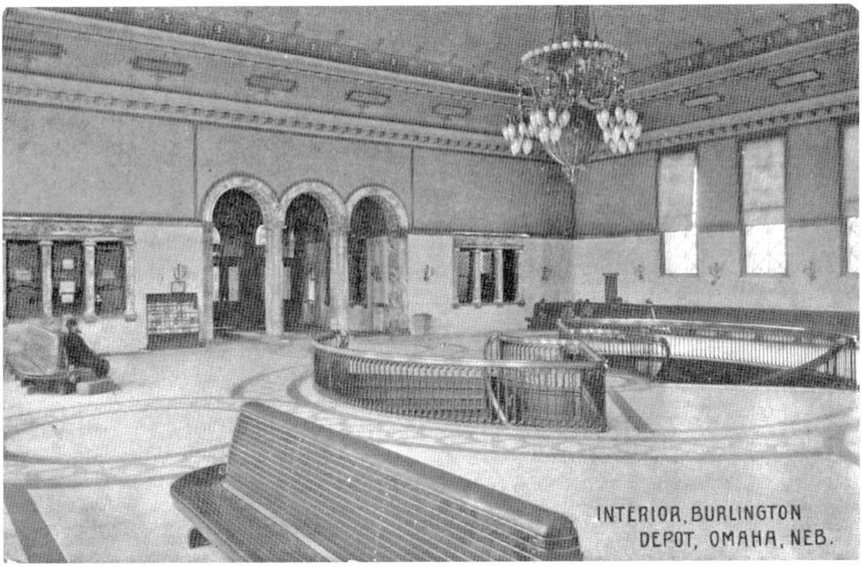

Burlington Station now houses KETV.

6. **Durham Museum**, 801 South 10th Street. Turn east onto Pacific, and go to 10th Street. Turn left onto 10th Street past the renovated Burlington Station, which now houses KETV, going about three blocks to the entrance of Durham Museum on the right.
7. **The Old Market**, 10–13th Streets, Jones to Harney Streets. Exit the Durham parking lot and turn right onto 10th Street. Go north about a block and turn left into the Old Market at Jackson Street. Park in either the large parking lot on the left, other nearby parking lots or on the streets (difficult). Explore the Old Market on foot. The **Bemis Center for the Contemporary Arts** and **Kaneko Omaha** are south of the parking lot while Howard Street, the market's main street, is a block north. Conclude the tour in the Old Market.

STATE HISTORICAL MARKERS

Poynter Hall

42nd and Dewey Avenue, University of Nebraska Medical Center

This marker, which is not on the tour, is located on the south wall of Poynter Hall and celebrates the 1902 founding of the University of Nebraska College of Medicine from the Omaha Medical College, a private medical school affiliated with the University of Nebraska. At first, classes were split between Lincoln and Omaha, but in 1909, the legislature approved this site for the college. The first building on the campus opened in 1913 (after escaping unharmed from the 1913 Easter tornado). It housed all medical school classes. The building is named for the college's longest-serving dean, Charles William McCorkle Poynter, and is now home to the department of psychiatry.[82]

HISTORIC SITES AND DISTRICTS

Field Club Historic District

32nd–36th Streets between Pacific and Center Streets

Field Club was founded in 1898 as Omaha's first country club. Omaha's U.S. Open Champion Johnny Goodman was a member, and golf legend Bobby Jones is among those who have played the club's golf course. The adjacent historic district includes a neighborhood of Gilded Age houses that is now in the National Register of Historic Places. In its first years, Field Club was a late nineteenth-century suburb on the city's southwest border, connected to Omaha by trolley. Many of the homes were designed by Omaha architect John McDonald.[83]

Gerald R. Ford Birth Site and Gardens

3202 Woolworth Avenue

In 1913, President Gerald R. Ford was born in Omaha as Leslie King and briefly lived in a home on this site that was owned by his grandparents, Charles Henry and Martha King. His mother, Dorothy Gardner, separated from his father, Leslie Lynch King, for domestic violence sixteen days after his birth. Eventually, Dorothy moved to Grand Rapids, Michigan, when she married Ford's stepfather and changed the boy's name. He grew up there as Gerald R. Ford.

After Ford became president, Omaha businessman James M. Paxson, who lived in the neighborhood, bought the vacant lot where the King house had stood and donated it to the city as a memorial. The Paxson Foundation funded the memorial and gardens, which were dedicated in 1977. The adjacent Gerald R. Ford Conservation Center operated by History Nebraska preserves and repairs historical and artistic artifacts. The center contains a small exhibit of Ford memorabilia. To make an appointment to tour the center, go to its website.[84]

Little Bohemia Historic District

South 13th Street, Hickory to William Streets

This district honors the Czech settlement of Omaha and includes colorful landmarks like the old Bohemian Café, now a craft brewery. Most buildings date to 1885–1900, and many are now being renovated.[85]

Sokol Auditorium

2234 South 13th Street

Sokol Auditorium in the Little Bohemia Historic District was built in 1926 to house Czech community social activities, including meetings for twenty-five Bohemian lodges, recreation activities and the gymnastics program that produced 1984 Olympic gold medalist James Hartung and Olympian Phil Cahoy. Today, Sokol is a popular venue for rock concerts and community activities.[86]

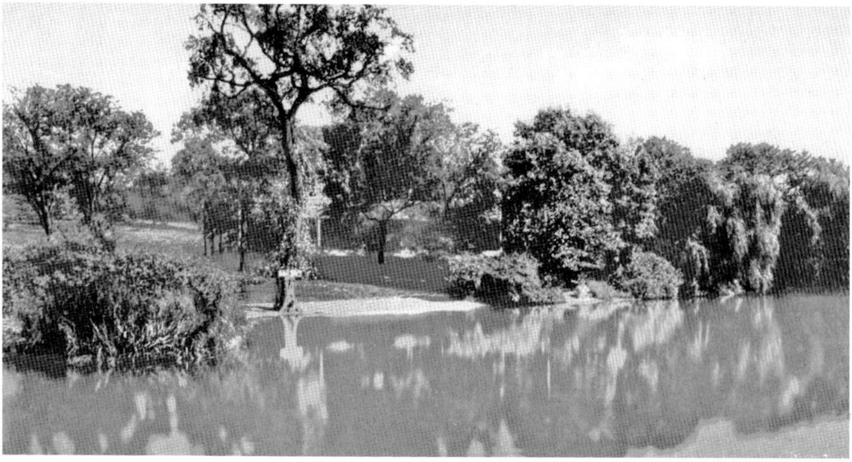

Hanscom Park Lagoon.

Historic Parks

Hanscom Park

1899 South 32nd Avenue

Hanscom Park is one of Omaha's oldest parks. Business leaders Andrew Hanscom and James Megeath donated the fifty-acre site to the city in 1872, and it was developed as a park in 1889—one of the first projects of the new Park Commission. The park, which is adjacent to the Ford Birth Site, features a lagoon and indoor tennis courts and is noted for its greenhouses that produce flowers for city parks. It is part of the parks and boulevard system that Omaha's early park landscape architects created to link city parks.[87]

Historic Churches

The varied immigrant communities that filled Near South neighborhoods a century ago founded churches celebrating their heritage. Here are some of them along with the "first churches" of various denominations that border downtown.

- **Assumption Ukrainian Catholic Church**, 16th and Martha Streets, was originally St. John's Greek Orthodox Church when the neighborhood was home to about two thousand Greek immigrants.

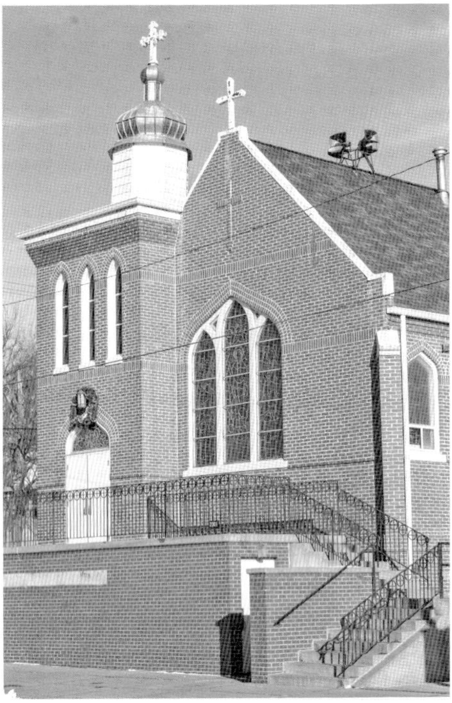

This page: Assumption Ukrainian Church was once St. John's Greek Orthodox Church. *Right photo by Carol McCabe.*

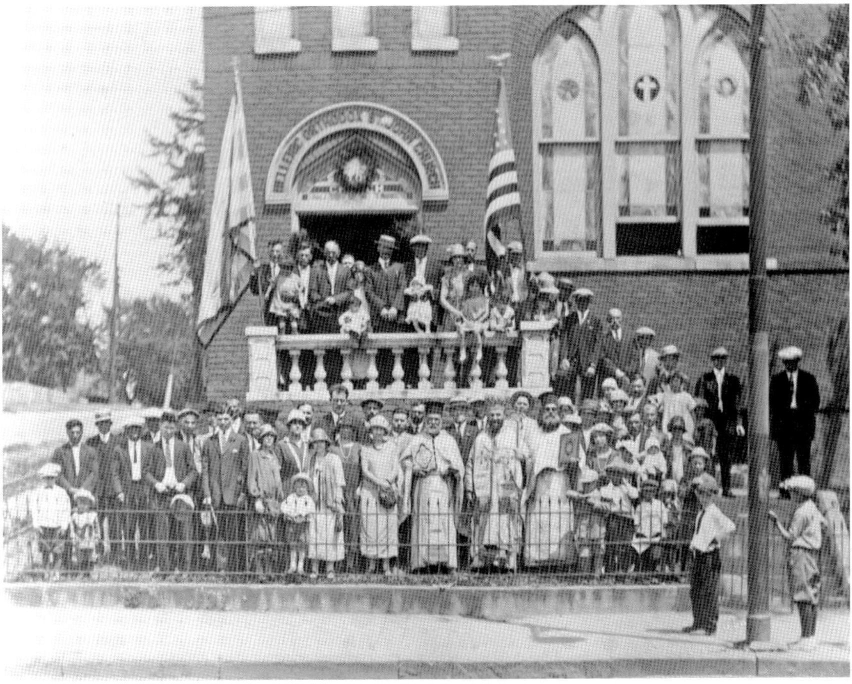

- **St. Joseph Church**, 1723 South 17th Street, was founded in 1886 to serve German and Polish immigrants.
- **Our Lady of Lourdes Church**, 2110 South 32nd Avenue, originally served suburban Hanscom Park, as it still does. Our Lady of Lourdes is paired with **St. Adalbert's Church**, and they are home to the Korean Catholic community.
- **St. Frances Cabrini Catholic Church**, 10th and William Streets, is in the heart of historic Little Italy and houses a statue of Saint Lucy displayed outside during the annual Santa Lucia Festival. Thomas Rogers Kimball designed the church in the Spanish style he adopted for St. Cecilia's Cathedral.[88]
- **First Baptist Church**, 27th Street and Park Avenue, was founded in 1855 and moved to this building in 1904.[89]
- **Dietz Memorial United Methodist Church**, 1423 South 10th Street, opened in 1889 and was originally St. Matthias Episcopal Church. It is an example of Romanesque Revival architecture and is in the National Register of Historic Places.
- **St. John's Greek Orthodox Church**, 602 Park Avenue, was founded in 1908 and moved from today's Assumption Ukrainian Catholic Church to this former Temple Israel building in 1951. Noted movie director Alexander Payne and his family are affiliated with St. John's.

Buildings in the National Register of Historic Places

There are numerous buildings in the National Register of Historic Places in this region. Some of the more noted structures include:

- **Anheuser-Busch Beer Depot**, 12th and Jones Streets
- **Joel Cornish House**, 1404 South 10th Street
- **Drake Court Historic District** 22nd and Jones Streets
- **Field Club Historic District**, 32nd–36th and Pacific-Center Streets
- **Normandie Apartments**, 1102 Park Avenue
- **Omaha Bolt Nut and Screw Building**, 1316 Jones Street
- **Omaha Rail and Commerce Historic District**, 15th–8th Streets between Jackson Street and the Union Pacific main line.
- **Poppleton Block**, 10th and Farnam Streets
- **Prague Hotel**, 1402 South 13th Street

HISTORIC OVERVIEW OF OMAHA'S TOP ATTRACTIONS

Information about Omaha's four top tourist attractions is readily available online and in other print sources. The following is a quick introduction to the history of the major sites in this area. All sites offer additional information. The region also includes numerous restaurants, coffeehouses and bars, many of them family run. The major sites all offer their own eating places, especially the Old Market, a center of the arts, food and street entertainment.

Lauritizen Gardens/Kenefick Park

100 Bancroft Street

Until 1982, Lauritzen Gardens, the city's major botanical garden, was a landfill. The gardens are named for the Lauritzen family of First National Bank. Today, it showcases numerous styles of gardens, including a rose garden, a Victorian garden, a children's garden, a Japanese garden and many more. An outdoor model train travels through the railroad garden past landmarks such as St. Cecilia's Cathedral, the Woodmen Tower and the Douglas County Courthouse. There are also statues of the prehistoric animals that once inhabited Nebraska. Kenefick Park, named for former Union Pacific president John Kenefick, features UP's Big Boy 4023, the world's largest steam locomotive, and Centennial No. 6900, the largest diesel-electric locomotive ever built. The locomotives are visible from Interstate 80.[90] Check the Lauritzen Gardens website for information on hours and admissions costs.

Omaha's Henry Doorly Zoo & Aquarium

3701 South 10th Street

When Omaha purchased the land to build Riverview Park in 1894, it decided that it should house a small zoo. Two years later, the zoo purchased its first animals, a moose, a grizzly bear and "moving fish." By 1901, the zoo included native stone quarters for bears, as well as pastures for deer, elk and buffalo. Other species such as bobcats, monkeys, wolves, deer and alligators came later. There was even a five-legged cow at one point.[91]

The zoo's history includes tragedies like the goring death of a caretaker and the drowning deaths of four children in the zoo's lagoon during a church picnic. During the Depression, the zoo struggled to feed its animals, but the WPA built cat cages and a monkey house. The zoo was forced to auction off two of its three lions during World War II.

After the war, Omaha explored ways to upgrade the zoo, which was little more than a menagerie. The breakthrough in creating today's world-class

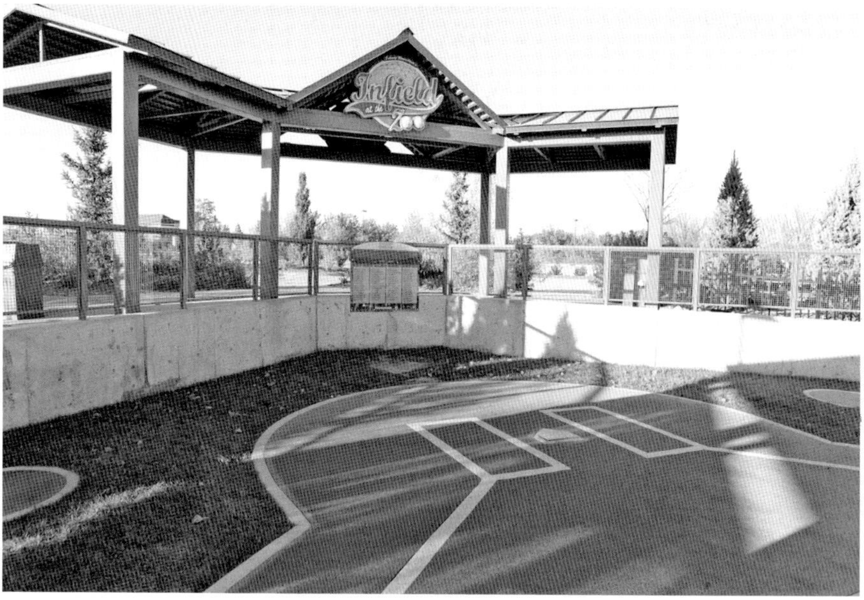

Infield at Henry Doorly Zoo celebrates College World Series history. *Photo by Mary Plambeck Cook.*

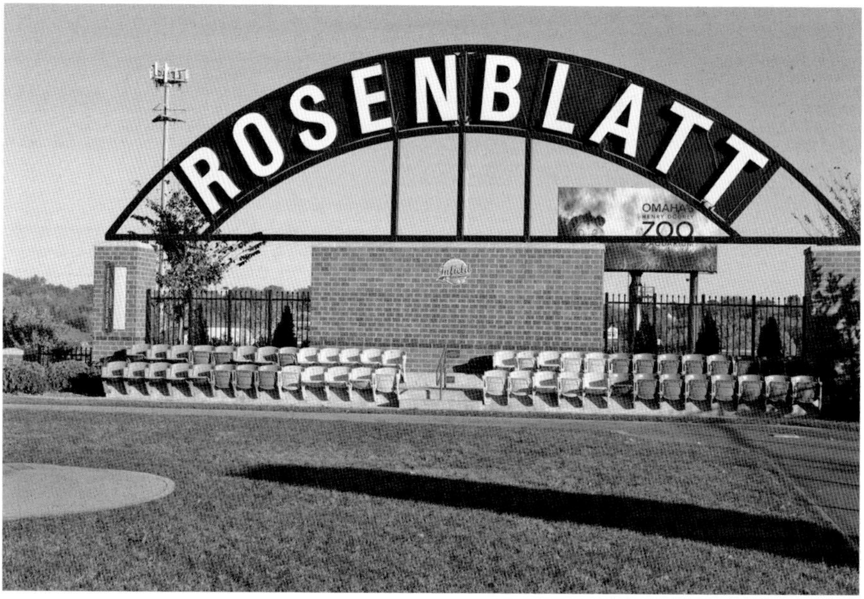

Sign of the former Rosenblatt Stadium, now part of the zoo. *Photo by Mary Plambeck Cook.*

zoo came in 1963, when Margaret Hitchcock Doorly donated $750,000 to transform the facility. She stipulated that the improved zoo be renamed for her late husband, the publisher of the *Omaha World-Herald*, and asked that animals be housed in settings as natural as possible.[92] Since then, Omaha has invested hundreds of millions of dollars in the zoo's spectacular exhibits, such as the Lied Jungle, the Walter and Suzanne Scott Aquarium, the Desert Dome, the African Grasslands and many more. The zoo, which in normal years attracts more than two million visitors, is also noted for its worldwide work in animal conservation. Check the website for information on hours and costs.

Durham Museum

801 South 10th Street

Omaha's major local historical museum is located in the large white Art Deco former Union Station, which evokes the city's railroad heritage. The station, which opened in 1931, was designed by Gilbert Stanley Underwood of Los Angeles and features terra-cotta walls. He said that the building tried to express the "distinctive character of the railroad: strength, power, masculinity." It served seven railroads and was noted both for technical innovations such as escalators and electric luggage conveyor belts and its lavish interior featuring marble columns and deep oak woodwork around windows and doors. It is in the National Register of Historic Places and part of the Omaha Rail and

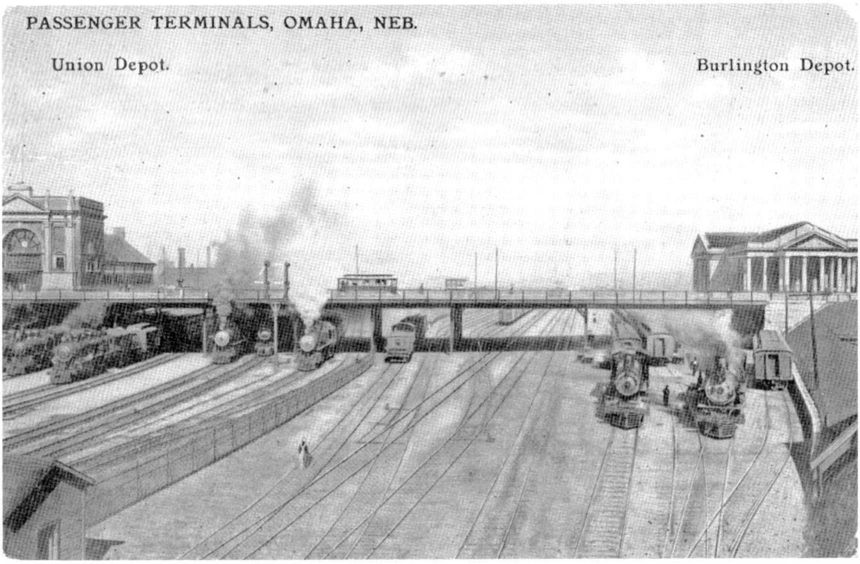

Railroad tracks between Union Station and Burlington Station.

Commerce Historic District.[93] The terminal's large passenger waiting room features statues representing the ten thousand passengers a day who passed through the station at its height in the 1940s.[94]

Union Pacific donated the station to the City of Omaha in 1973 after Amtrak took over passenger service in 1971. Two years later, Western Heritage Museum opened. It was closed in 1995 for a $22 million renovation project largely funded by Omaha philanthropists Charles and Margre Durham, for whom the museum was renamed.[95]

Durham features walk-through displays of Union Pacific equipment; a large model train; replicas of early stores, including the Buffett Grocery Store (run by the family of billionaire Warren Buffett); and a turn-of-the-twentieth-century classroom in addition to the magnificent Byron Reed coin collection. Reed was a prominent realtor and politician.[96] Researchers can access important collections of photos of Omaha. Check the website for hours and admissions costs

The Old Market

10th–13th and Jones-Harney Streets

This local gem, the center of Omaha's arts community, barely escaped destruction after the Old City Market closed in 1964. "Market Dies and so Does an Era," said the headline on a *World-Herald* story about the sale of three lots to owners who planned to turn the old fruit and vegetable warehouses into a parking lot. The area had fallen victim to chain grocery stores that bought their produce elsewhere.[97]

However, Sam Mercer, an Omaha native who was an attorney in Paris, had a different vision for the Old Market buildings his family owned. In January 1968, he announced plans to turn the area into a commercial area. Early businesses included the French Café, an art gallery called the Creative Person and Edison Exposure, and a theater.[98] Gradually, the Old Market overcame a reputation as a hangout for hippies and drug users as it began to attract upscale businesses and restaurants, festivals, art galleries and studios.

Omaha native Ree Schonlau Kaneko played a key role in founding the two most important arts attractions in the Old Market. The **Bemis Center for Contemporary Arts** at 12th and Leavenworth Streets opened in 1981 in the old Bemis Bag warehouse. It offers residencies in free studio space to promising young artists worldwide and gained an international reputation. Its galleries are open to the public. Check the website for times.

Kaneko Omaha at 11th and Jones Streets is a major gallery in another renovated warehouse featuring the world-famous sculptures of Jun Kaneko (husband of Ree) and special exhibits of contemporary art, as well as programs designed to stimulate creativity. Check the website for more information.

Other galleries that display the work of local artists include the **Artists' Cooperative Gallery** at 405 South 11th Street. Google the Old Market for names and hours of other galleries in the area or simply explore the area.

Today, Omahans who enjoy the market's urban vibe occupy the loft apartments above many of the stores and restaurants. They, along with residents of nearby converted warehouses and commercial buildings, have turned the downtown/market area into a residential space with a population of at least twenty-five thousand. But there's at least one reminder of the market's produce warehouse roots—the popular farmer's market that draws large crowds on summer Saturdays. Street musicians and horse-drawn carriage rides have long been part of the area's ambiance. Check the websites of various Old Market attractions for information about attractions and hours.

THINGS TO DO

All four of the major tourism sites are destinations, some containing multiple entertainment, dining and shopping opportunities. But go beyond the big four to explore smaller areas, coffeehouses, bars, breweries and ethnic restaurants. Visit a park or walk through a neighborhood of period houses like Field Club. Get a sense of life in historic Omaha.

7
SOUTH OMAHA

Travel to Mexico without leaving Omaha. Head to downtown South Omaha to enter a world of authentic Mexican restaurants, specialty stores and music with colorful street murals. Visit the old Polish Home converted to El Museo Latino to absorb Latinx arts and culture. It's just the latest evolution of this traditional melting pot area.

South Omaha has had a character of its own since 1883, when cattle baron Alexander Hamilton Swan of Wyoming and six prominent Omaha businessmen founded the Union Stockyards in a rural area just south of Omaha. A year later, they platted a separate town, South Omaha, which was incorporated two years later and remained independent until Omaha annexed it in 1915. By then, it had forty thousand residents, many of them immigrants from southern and eastern Europe who came to work in meatpacking.

The massive stockyards, once the nation's largest, closed in 1999 as the industry decentralized. Most packinghouses are gone, but there are reminders of the days when meatpacking was Omaha's dominant industry in the old stockyards area between L and Q Streets from about 30th to 36th Streets. A series of markers outside the Livestock Exchange Building details the history of the Stockyards. Park and walk through them.[99]

But today's vibrant South Omaha belongs to the Latino community. There's always something happening along South 24th Street in the historic business district buildings now displaying signs in Spanish and English. Brush up on your Spanish and enjoy the adventure.

Life in Meatpacking

The stockyards attracted thousands of immigrants to a new life in South Omaha. In 1892, *World-Herald* columnist Elia Peattie offered the following memorable portrait of the process they followed to turn cattle into beef:

> *Nearly 2,000 men and women are engaged in Cudahy's packinghouse. And the stranger who visits there could easily believe there are more, for the place, vast as it is, seems swarming the men, boys and girls who, over and over, with a swiftness almost incredible, do the same thing every day of the year....*
>
> *The work is unrelenting from the time the whistle blows in the morning, till night. The young Bohemian who stands with his legs well apart and his fine arms half bared out at the end of a chute where the cattle run from the brown hillside, never alters from the steady down-falling of his big hammer. And each fall of that hammer knocks into insensibility a "beef." From the moment it descends with its unerring aim, the cow or steer ceases to be anything but a "beef," although for several seconds it lives. As a precautionary measure against suffering, its throat is also cut and then a moment later, it is swung up, its hide pulled off as neatly and quite as quietly as a lady pulls a glove from her hand, and down the carcass, cutting cleanly and opening up the carcass, goes the keen knife.*

Peattie went on to describe the rest of the graphic details of the slaughter process, such as entrails spilling out.

In other columns, Peattie described the modest neighborhoods where the immigrants lived, most now home to the newest generation of immigrants. Her columns of life in the city's rich and poor areas are a social portrait of Gilded Age Omaha.

SUGGESTED TOUR ROUTE

This route includes navigation directions. The remainder of the chapter gives information on sites, organized by category. Within categories such as state historic markers or landmark buildings, sites are listed by their order

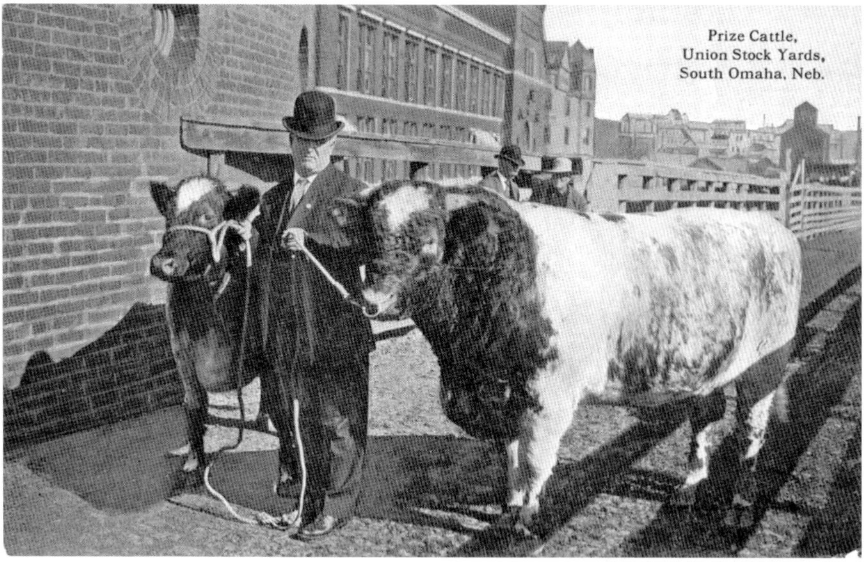

Postcard of a man with his prize cow at the stockyards.

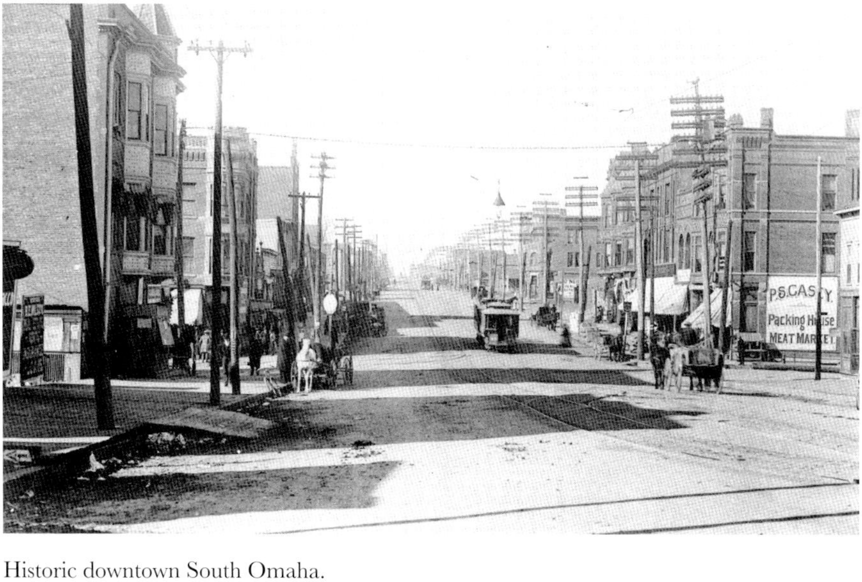

Historic downtown South Omaha.

in the tour. This chapter also includes information on scattered landmarks, such as ethnic churches and Miguel Keith Park, which are not included in this tour route.

1. **Vinton Street Commercial District**, 17th, Elm and Vinton Streets. Begin route at 16th and Vinton Streets, although the historic commercial district officially begins at 17th Street. Turn right onto Vinton and go west to 24th Street, passing galleries, ethnic businesses and street murals. At 24th Street, turn left onto L Street.
2. **South Omaha Main Street Historic District**, South 24th Street, M–O Street. Drive south on 24th Street to downtown South Omaha. Note landmarks such as **St. Luke's Lutheran Church**, **St. Martin of Tours Episcopal Church** and **South High** on the east side of the street. Landmarks along this main street include the **South Omaha Post Office, Roseland Apartments**, the old **Packers National Bank** and the former **South Omaha City Hall**. Consider stopping to walk the area to savor the area's ambiance before driving south to Q Street and turning right onto it.
3. **Metropolitan Community College** (MCC), South 27th and Q Streets. Take Q Street west to the entrance to the MCC campus and go north on 27th Street to Ed Babe Gomez Boulevard and then turn left and follow it to 30th Street, passing markers commemorating the history of the Omaha stockyards. Follow 30th to L Street, passing the Livestock Exchange Building.
4. **Livestock Exchange Building**, 4920 South 30th Street. Consider parking at the Livestock Exchange Building to see it and to walk through the stockyard markers. At 30th and L, turn around and retrace the route to Q Street and then go west to 36th Street.
5. **St. Mary's Church and Cemetery/Supermercado**, 36th and Q Streets. St. Mary's Cemetery is on the south side of Q Street, just east of St. Mary's Church. The Supermercado on the north side of Q features a large mural depicting the history of South Omaha on its west wall. Turn right onto 36th Street, go north to L Street and turn right onto it.

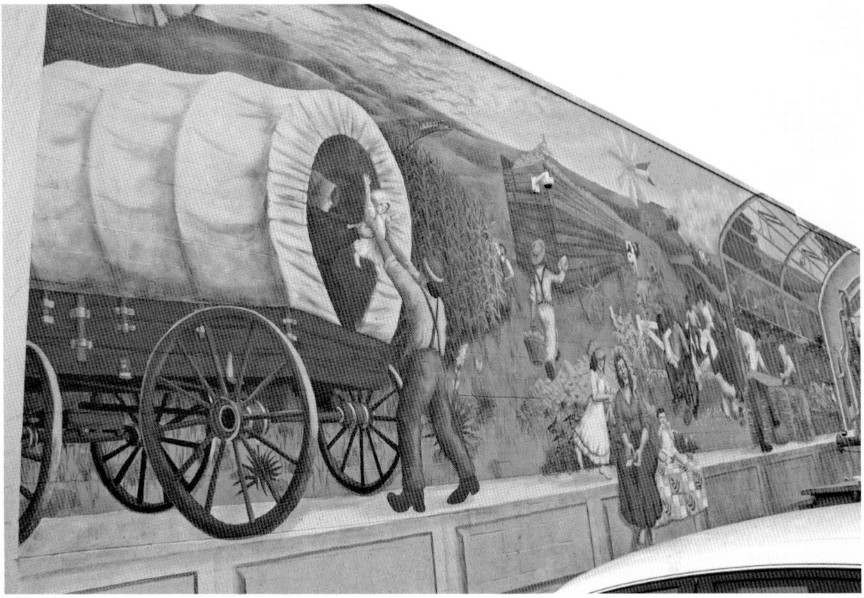

This street mural depicts South Omaha's history. *Photo by Carol Mccabe.*

6. **El Museo Latino**, 4701 South 25th Street. Drive east on L past the Stockyards Plaza, and the Stockyards Business Park. Johnny's Café, the classic Stockyards steakhouse, is south of L at 27th Street. Turn right on 25th Street to visit El Museo Latino, located in the old Polish Home. Continue east on L.
7. **South Omaha Veterans Memorial Bridge**, 13th and L Streets. Drive east on L to 13th and turn south onto 13th Street at the South Omaha Bridge to Council Bluffs.
8. **Mount Vernon Gardens**, 13th and W Streets. Turn left off 13th Street at the second entrance into Mount Vernon Gardens for a panoramic view of the Missouri River. Return to 13th Street, go north to U Street and turn left onto it.
9. **Brown Park**, 5708 South 15th Street. Go west on U to Brown Park. The park features the recently renovated historic John Stella Ballfield. Complete the tour by driving west on U to 24th Street.

HISTORICAL MARKERS AND LANDMARKS

Nebraska Historical Markers

South Omaha People, Metropolitan Community College
South 27th and Q Streets
This marker on the MCC campus located in the old stockyards area celebrates the people of many backgrounds who came to work here.[100]

Historic Districts

Vinton Street Commercial Historic District
17th–Elm and Vinton Streets
This district along Vinton Street from 17th to Elm Streets is adjacent to historic Sheelytown, where Irish, Polish and eastern European immigrants lived. Today, it is home to small stores, restaurants and a few art galleries. It was added to the National Register of Historic Places in 2006.[101] Access it from 16th Street.

South Omaha Main Street Historic District
South 24th Street, M–O Streets
This district is home to numerous historic buildings and was added to the National Register of Historic Places in 1989. Some of these buildings include:

- **Packer's National Bank Building**, 4939 South 24th Street, designed by architect Thomas Rogers Kimball in the 1890s to house the bank that was tied closely to the growth of the stockyards. The bank left the building in 1979, and it was renovated to house offices and apartments.
- **Roseland Theater Apartments**, 4934 South 24th Street, was a movie theater from its construction in the 1920s until the 1980s, when it was converted to commercial use and apartments.
- Former **South Omaha City Hall**, 5002 South 24th Street, was built in the 1890s and designed by architect John Latenser.[102]
- **South Omaha Post Office**, 4720 South 24th Street, is one of the thirty-two notable buildings in the historic district and remains a hub of downtown South Omaha.

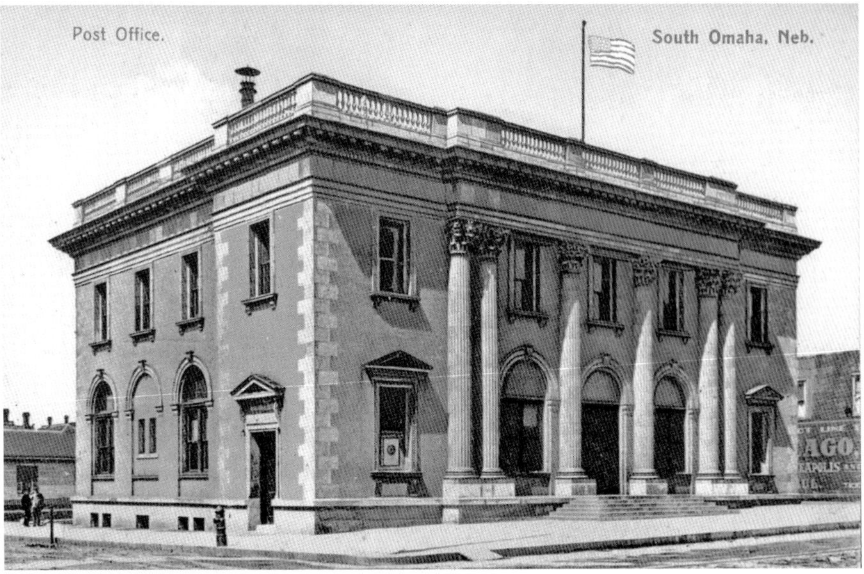

Historic South Omaha Post Office.

Historic Buildings/Museums

Livestock Exchange Building/Stockyards Markers

4920 South 30th Street

The great stockyards are gone, but this 1926 building designed by George Prinz is a reminder of the boom era of the stockyards and packinghouses. Not only did it formerly house livestock commission offices and other businesses related to the yards, but it also was a shopping center with a doctor's office, barbershop, clothing store and other businesses. Today, it houses offices, apartments and One World Health Center, but the large ballrooms on the top two stories still host social events such as weddings.[103] Outside the Livestock Exchange Building, a series of markers along 30th Street recount the history of the stockyards.

El Museo Latino

4701 South 25th Street

This museum, located in the old Polish Home since 1997, celebrates Latino art, history and culture and is one of the few such museums in the Midwest. It is noted for its traveling exhibits, as well as its permanent collections and community activities. The *U*-shaped Romanesque Revival building was built in

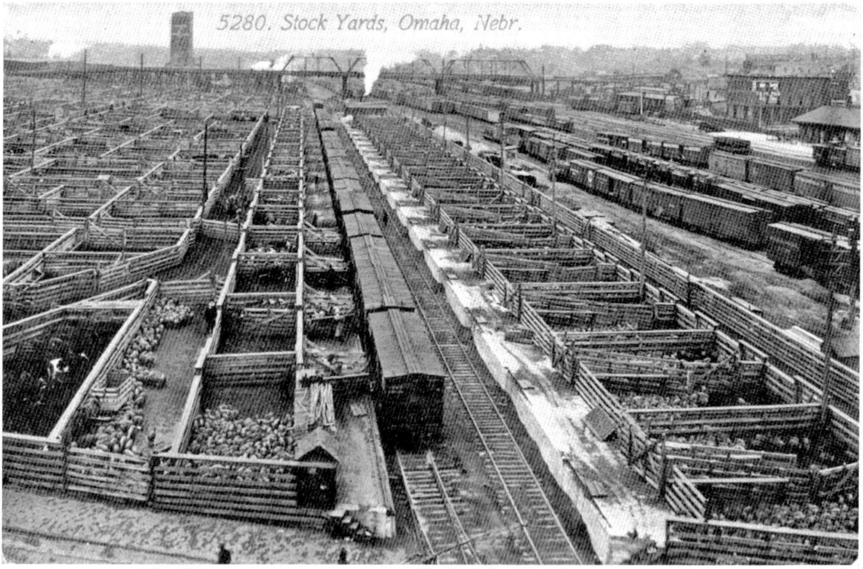

Pens in the Omaha yards.

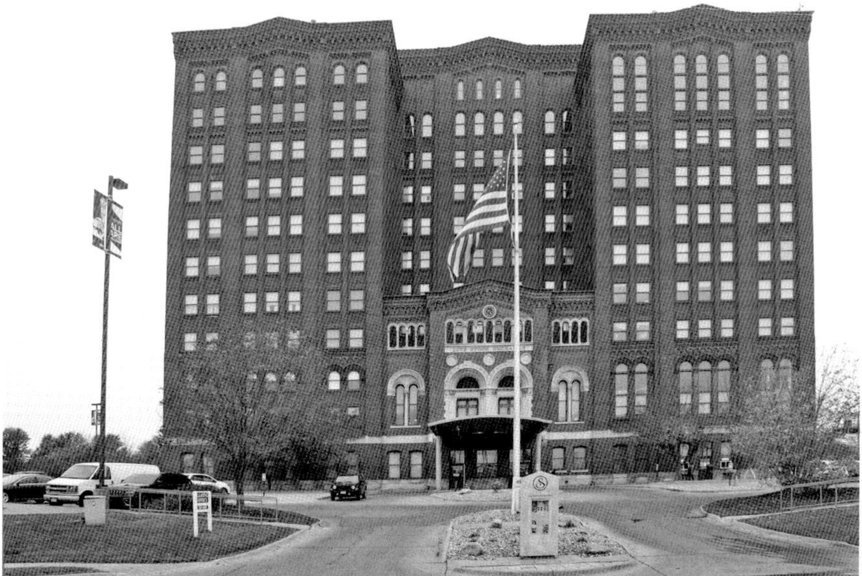

Livestock Exchange Building. *Photo by Carol McCabe.*

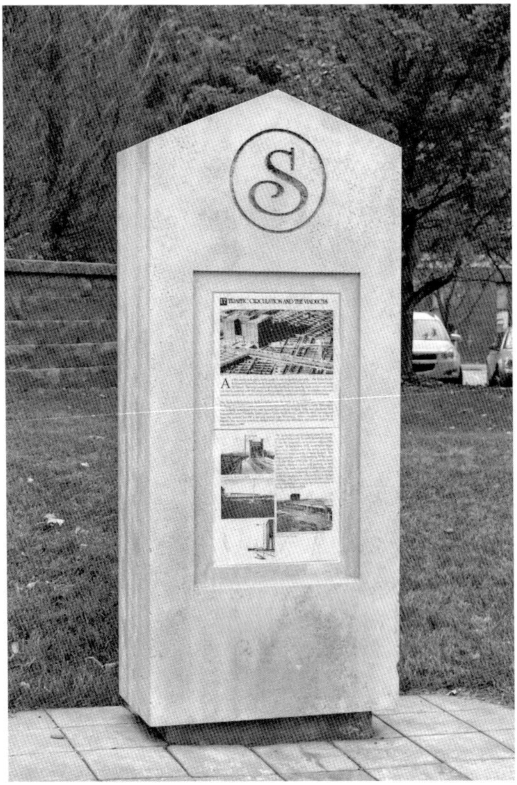

This page: Markers tell the history of the Omaha Stockyards. *Photo by Carol McCabe.*

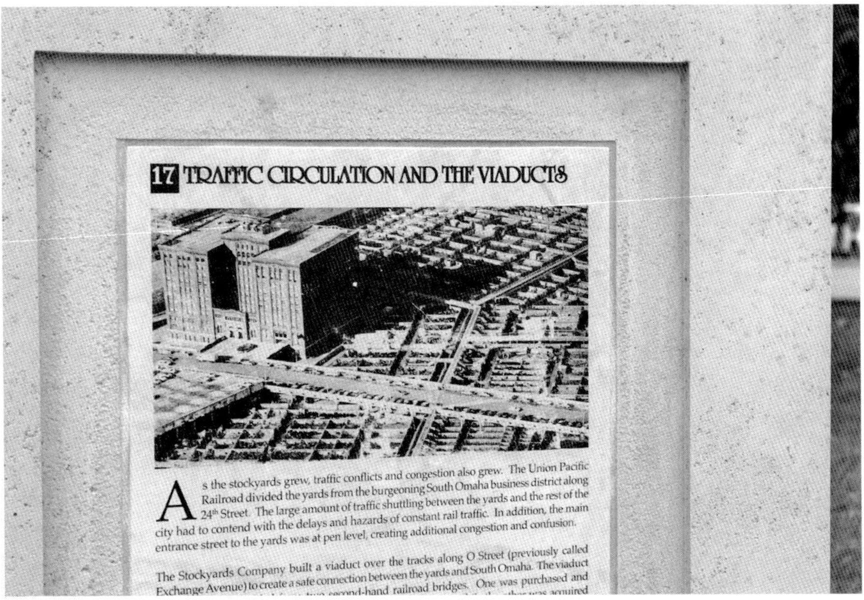

1887 as South Central School. It became the Polish Home in 1936 and was a venue for educational and social events. Check the website for hours and information about exhibits.[104]

Historic Parks

Mount Vernon Gardens
6011 West 13th Street
This spot offers a panoramic view of the Missouri River. It opened in 1931 and was designed to resemble George Washington's Mount Vernon Estate in Virginia. Landscape architect George Hood followed the exact layout and looks of Mount Vernon in the 1920s. This is a popular location for outdoor weddings.[105]

Brown Park
5708 South 15th Street
This park contains a ballfield that is more than one hundred years old and hosted games in which Ty Cobb played. Babe Ruth and Lou Gehrig played at nearby League Park at 15th and Vinton during a 1927 barnstorming tour. The Brown Park field has been renovated and is named for John Stella, a longtime American Legion baseball coach.[106]

Miguel Keith Park
30th and Y Streets
This park, which is not included in the tour route, honors South Omaha marine lance corporal Miguel Keith, who won the Medal of Honor during the Vietnam War. It features a statue of him.

Historic Bridge

South Omaha Veterans Memorial Bridge
13th and L Streets
The original South Omaha Bridge opened in 1936 to provide a direct route across the Missouri River to the Omaha Stockyards and was a toll bridge until 1947. It was listed in the National Register of Historic Places in 1992 but was removed after it was torn down in 2010 and replaced by today's bridge. It was renamed in 1995.[107]

Historic Ethnic Churches

South Omaha is home to numerous ethnic churches because the many groups that poured into the area wanted their own nationality congregations even when they shared a common faith such as Catholicism. Many are named for favorite old country saints and feature statues and windows reflecting their heritage. The following are some of these churches, most just noted with their addresses and national backgrounds unless they are in the National Register of Historic Places or there is some unique feature.

Immaculate Conception Catholic Church

2708 South 24th Street

This historic Polish church in the National Register of Historic Places was built in 1926. Just west of the church is a recreation center that contains one of the last church-run bowling alleys. It was designed by Omaha architect Jacob Nachitgall.[108]

St. Martin of Tours Episcopal Church

2312 J Street

This church was founded in 1876 and is listed in the National Register of Historic Places. It is also an Omaha Landmark. Its architecture evokes the church styles of the Middle Ages.[109]

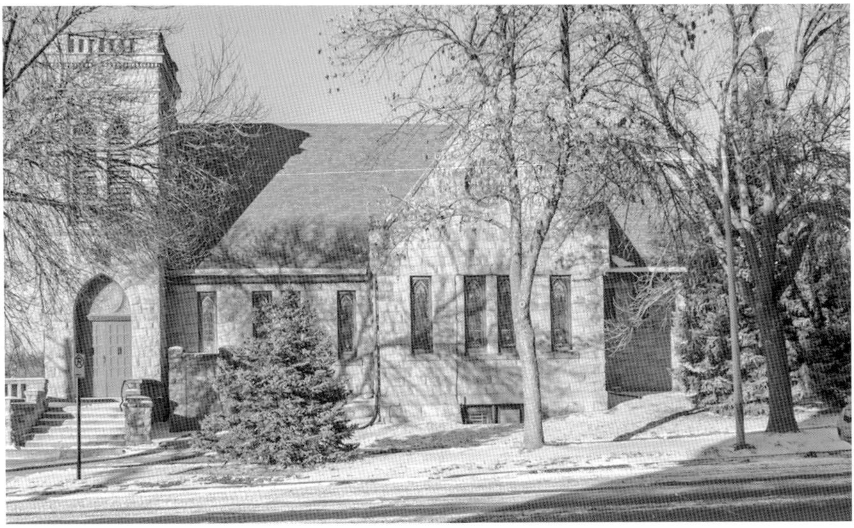

St. Martin of Tours Episcopal Church. *Photo by Carol McCabe.*

Bible Church
23rd and J Streets
This church began as a synagogue and then became Wheeler Presbyterian Church before assuming its present identity. Omaha formerly had numerous small synagogues that consolidated into today's three major Jewish congregations.[110]

Our Lady of Guadalupe
2310 O Street
This is Omaha's largest Mexican parish, and its grounds reflect that heritage. The parish opened in 1919 and moved to this location in 1951. The building has been enlarged, reflecting the influx of Hispanic people into South Omaha in recent years. Note the colorful murals on streets, including one at 24th and N that depicts Our Lady of Guadalupe, patron saint of Mexico.[111]

St. Mary's Catholic Church and Cemetery
36th and Q Streets
This Irish parish is noted for the large Celtic window that speaks to its heritage. Just east of the church is St. Mary's Cemetery, one of Omaha's oldest Catholic cemeteries. Because the Catholic Church had consecrated the land, many early Catholics used it as a burial ground even though a permit to do so was not issued until 1873.[112]

A few of the other churches connected with the area's many ethnic groups include:

- **St. Stanislaus Catholic Church**, 4002 J Street, a Polish nationality parish
- **Sts. Peter and Paul Catholic Church**, 36th and X Streets, a Croatian nationality parish
- **St. Cross Romanian Orthodox Church**, 33rd and R Streets, is closed but its architecture speaks to the neighborhood's old Romanian community.
- **St. Nicholas Serbian Orthodox Church**, 5050 Harrison Street

Street Murals

Throughout South Omaha, buildings are decorated with colorful murals too numerous to mention. Here are a few to watch for:

- **Louie M Burger Lust**, 1718 Vinton Street
- **Our Lady of Guadalupe**, 24th and N Streets
- **Supermercado, History of South Omaha**, 36th and Q Streets
- **Donahue's Bar**, 33rd and L Streets, depicts events in South Omaha's labor and ethnic group history.

THINGS TO DO

Tour South Omaha on a nice day so that you can walk around downtown enjoying the street life. Eat at one of the numerous family-run Mexican restaurants, and plan several excursions to sample more. Spend some time in the Vinton Street district visiting the small galleries and specialty shops, and for a change from Mexican food, drop by Louie M's Burger Lust, an area institution, or treat yourself to a steak dinner at Johnny's, the classic stockyards restaurant whose décor features pictures of cattle and other reminders of the livestock industry that built the area.

8

BENSON AND WEST OMAHA

While this book focuses on Omaha's historic core, one of the city's must-see sites, Boys Town, is just west of 132nd Street. We've packaged it with Benson, one of the city's first suburbs, because it's easy to drive west to historic sites there. En route from Benson, stop at the lovely Heron Haven nature center.

West Omaha is not one undifferentiated mass, although the appellation implies this. Beginning in the 1960s, Omaha began expanding rapidly to the west, and eventually, it annexed two of its former suburbs, Millard and Elkhorn. There's no agreement on where today's West Omaha begins, but many would say it is west of 120th Street. The construction of Interstate 80 encouraged the growth of residential and commercial areas ever farther west.

Even though they are a considerable distance from other sites in this book, the Boys Town Hall of History and the museum of local Jewish history run by the Nebraska Jewish Historical Society, are important stops for local history enthusiasts. Temple Israel, Nebraska's oldest Jewish congregation, is part of the new Tri-Faith Center, which also includes a Muslim mosque and Christian church. All of these sites are located close to each other on the east side of 132nd between Dodge and Pacific Streets. Farther west, Elkhorn marks a spot on the historic Lincoln Highway, and farther south is the Standing Bear marker on Papio Lake, neither on the tour route.

A Tragedy at Krug Park

At today's Gallagher Park on the east side of Benson, summer finds kids splashing in its popular swimming pool that includes a wading pool and waterslide. Residents walk their dogs, and families enjoy the playground and ballfield. There's little evidence of the period from 1895 to 1930, when the site was privately operated Krug Park, Omaha's most popular amusement park, which included a penny arcade, seventy-two-horse merry-go-round, dance pavilion and ice cream parlor. Before Prohibition, there also was a beer garden.

One of Krug Park's major attractions was its Big Dipper roller coaster. However, on July 24, 1930, tragedy struck as the ride's four connected cars were climbing the thirty-five-foot incline. A loose bolt caused the lead car's brake shoe to get caught in the car's rear wheels, plunging the cars thirty-five-feet downward. Four riders were killed and seventeen were injured. At the time, it was the nation's deadliest roller coaster crash.

Inspectors blamed the accident on poor upkeep, and Omaha decreed that no roller coasters would be allowed to operate in the city. Krug Park was sold, but it never overcame the notoriety of the tragedy. It closed for good in 1940.

In 1955, the city reopened the site as Gallagher Park, in honor of Rachel and Paul Gallagher, who helped finance the transformation. Rachel Gallagher devoted her life to protecting and improving Omaha's parks.*

* "Krug Park," *Omaha Magazine*.

SUGGESTED TOUR ROUTE

This tour route includes navigation directions. The remainder of the chapter gives information on sites, organized by category. Within categories such as state historic markers or landmark buildings, sites are listed by their order in the tour. A few places outside our route, such as the Nebraska Historical Markers for the Lincoln Highway at Elkhorn and Standing Bear to the south, that are not included on the route.

1. **Gallagher Park/Krug Park**, 2936 North 52nd Street. Begin your tour here and go west on the Radial Highway to 58th Street. Turn north at the light and go through the slight curve onto Maple Street into the Benson commercial area.
2. **Historic Benson**, Maple Street, 58th–64th Streets. Drive west on Maple through Benson or walk down this renovated historic district of restaurants, entertainment venues and unique shops. Note historic buildings, including the **Masonic Temple**, 5901 Maple Street; **Bank of Benson**, 6108 Maple Street; **B.H. Post Building**, 6214 Maple Street; and the **Benson U.S. Post Office**, 6223 Maple Street.
3. **Heron Haven**, 11809 Old Maple Road. Continue west on Maple to Heron Haven, turning right onto 120th Street. Take a sharp right at Ione Werthman Road and drive east into the nature sanctuary. Return to 120th and turn right onto Old Maple Road. Go west to 132nd Street and turn left onto it.
4. **Boys Town Entrance**, 132nd and Walsh Drive. Turn right off 132nd at the entrance sign to Boys Town. Drive west into Boys Town. Stop at the visitor's center at 136th and Flanagan Boulevard for information on sites including the **Dowd Memorial Chapel**, the **House of History** and **Father Flanagan Historic House**. Follow signs to Sheehan Parkway and return to the access road to 132nd Street and turn right onto it.
5. **Nebraska Jewish Historical Society**, 333 South 132nd Street. Take 132nd Street south to the Jewish Community Center on the east side of the street. Turn left into it. The museum is inside the center.
6. **Tri-Faith Center**, 132nd and Pacific Streets/**Temple Israel**. Return to 132nd Street, turn left and continue south past 132nd Street. Turn east into the entrance of the Tri-Faith Campus to find Temple Israel.

STATE HISTORIC MARKERS

Nebraska School for the Deaf

3223 North 45th Street

The legislature established the Nebraska School for the Deaf in 1867, and it opened two years later at 22nd Street and St. Mary's Avenue. Its first principal was William DeCoursey French, a deaf man. It moved to this location in 1871 and closed in 1998 due to the enrollment of deaf children in public schools. During its 129-year history, it educated more than two thousand deaf students. Their achievements included winning the 1931 Class A state boys basketball team championship.[113] This marker is in a residential area east of Benson and is not on the tour.

Father Flanagan's Boys' Home

2 Flanagan Boulevard, Boys Town

This marker on the Boys Town campus celebrates this internationally known home for homeless, abandoned and neglected boys that Father Edward Flanagan founded in 1917. Boys Town began with five boys at a house at 25th and Dodge—two from juvenile court and two homeless newsboys. In 1921, Flanagan bought Overlook Farm, then about ten miles outside of Omaha, the nucleus of today's campus.[114]

Boys Town became internationally famous with the help of a 1938 Academy Award–winning movie starring Spencer Tracy as Father Flanagan and Mickey Rooney as one of the boys. Today, Boys Town serves both boys and girls on the main campus and at other sites nationally. Locally, it also operates the Boys Town Research Hospital specializing in hearing disorders.

Chief Standing Bear

Papio Lake 16 Road South

This marker celebrates the history of the Ponca Indians and their most famous member, Chief Standing Bear, and his landmark trial. In 1877, the federal government forced the Poncas to move from their northeast Nebraska home to Oklahoma, a five-hundred-mile journey on foot. In 1879, Standing Bear was arrested after he returned to Nebraska illegally to bury his son. At Standing Bear's trial in Omaha District Court, the judge decided for the first time that American Indians were persons within the meaning of the law.[115] Today, Chief Standing Bear is considered a human rights pioneer, and his statue represents Nebraska in the U.S. Capitol's Statuary Hall. This marker is not on the tour.

Lincoln Highway at Elkhorn

Old Lincoln Highway between North 192nd and North 180th

This three-mile brick segment of highway was once on the route of the Lincoln Highway. In 1913, the private Lincoln Highway Association was founded to develop a paved toll-free highway from New York to San Francisco. This section between Omaha and Elkhorn was mapped in 1913 and was originally unpaved. In 1920, it was paved with a concrete underlay and brick surfacing. In 1930, the highway's route was changed, bypassing this segment. It is in the National Register of Historic Places because it is a well-preserved example of early twentieth-century road construction.[116] This marker is not on the tour.

HISTORIC AREAS

Benson

Benson was founded in 1887 by Erastus Benson, a land speculator who founded the town on a farm he purchased from Edward Creighton. It was along Military Avenue about nine miles west of Omaha, eventually becoming one of the streetcar suburbs like Dundee and Florence. Omaha annexed it in 1917. Today, its commercial area goes west on Maple Street from about 58th Street to about 64th Street. Many of its old brick stores have become boutiques, bars, restaurants and entertainment venues that some compare to the Old Market.

Benson retains the feel of a turn-of the-twentieth-century small town with its own high school, post office, public library, churches and nearby residential area as well as a variety of churches. Walk down Maple to enjoy today's revitalized area. Historic buildings include:

- **Masonic Temple**, 5901 Maple Street
- **Bank of Benson**, 6108 Maple Street
- **B.H. Post Building**, 6214 Maple Street
- **Benson U.S. Post Office**, 6223 Maple Street[117]

Historic Parks

Gallagher Park/Krug Park

2936 North 52nd Street

Today's Gallagher Park was founded in 1895 by Charles Tietz, a German American immigrant, as a beer garden with amusement rides. He sold it to the

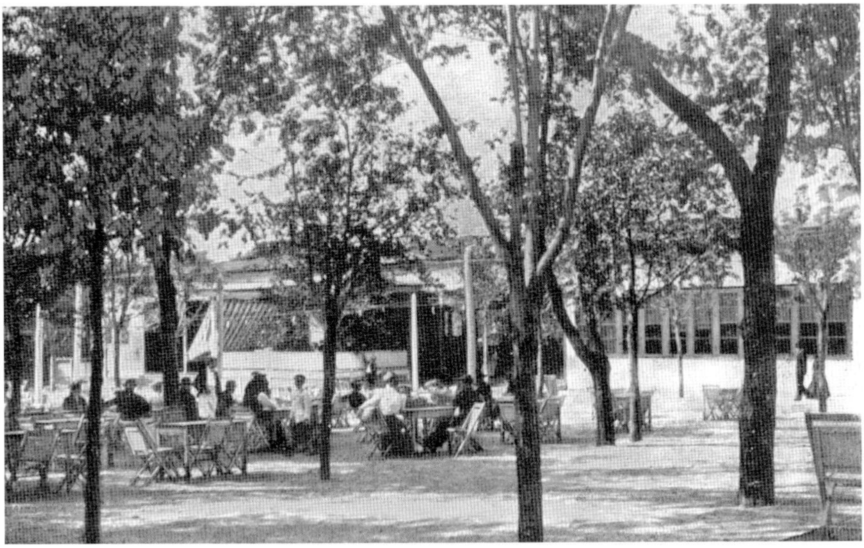

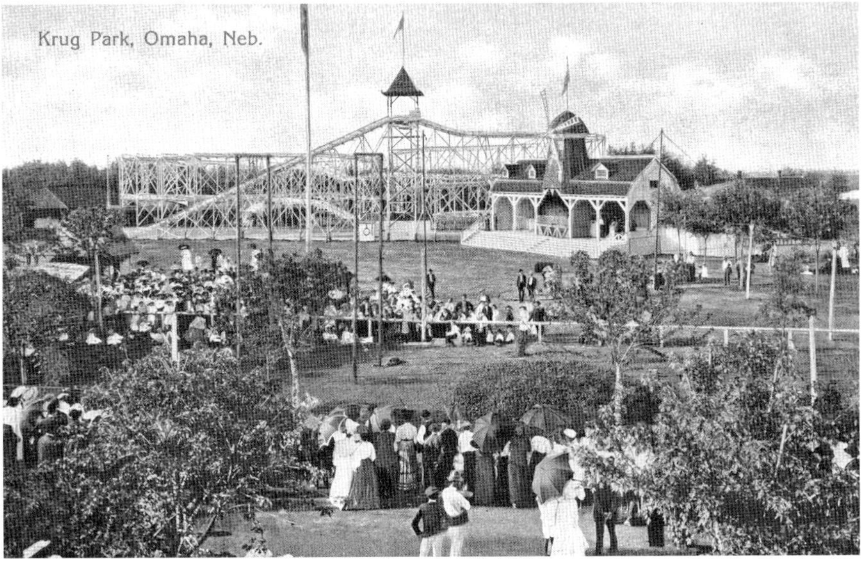

Krug Park was famous for its roller coaster and became today's Gallagher Park.

Frederick Krug Brewing Company in 1902. Rides included a tunnel of love, an ice cream parlor and a hot air balloon. In 1918, a ballroom, swimming pools, a waterfall, a wave machine and a bathhouse were added. Krug Park is famous for the nation's most deadly roller coaster accident up to 1930 when the park's Big Dipper roller coaster crashed. Four cars of children and teens plunged to the ground, killing four passengers and injuring seventeen. The city then banned roller coasters.

Krug Park closed in 1940 but reopened in 1955 as a traditional city park, named for Rachel and Paul Gallagher, who contributed to the renovation. Rachel Gallagher founded Friends of the Parks and devoted much of her life to crusading for Omaha's parks.[118]

Heron Haven

11809 Old Maple Road

Although this wetland sanctuary opened in 2015, it can be considered historic because it preserved one of the Big Papillion Creek's last oxbow wetlands. The thirty-acre site includes a visitor center, trails, bridges over wet areas and an education center housing a library and small nature museum. Check the sanctuary's website for more information on hours.

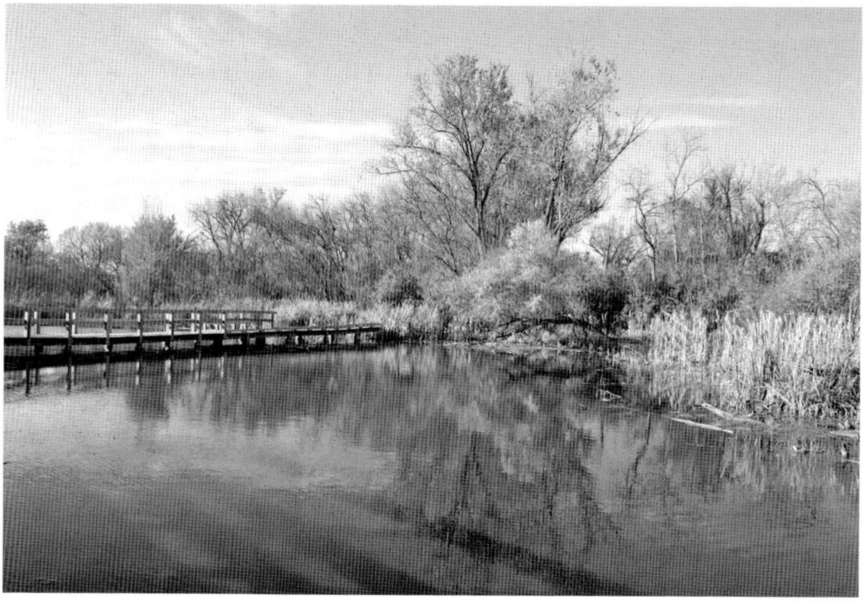

Heron Haven is a wetlands sanctuary. *Photo by Carol McCabe.*

Museums

Boys Town Hall of History

Former Dining Hall, Boys Town Campus

This museum features exhibits that present the history and development of Boys Town. Audio and video presentations interpret both past work and current programs nationally. Artifacts on display include Spencer Tracy's Oscar for portraying Father Flanagan in the movie *Boys Town*. Today's visitors can take virtual visits as well. Check the Boys Town website for more information on when it is open to visitors.[119]

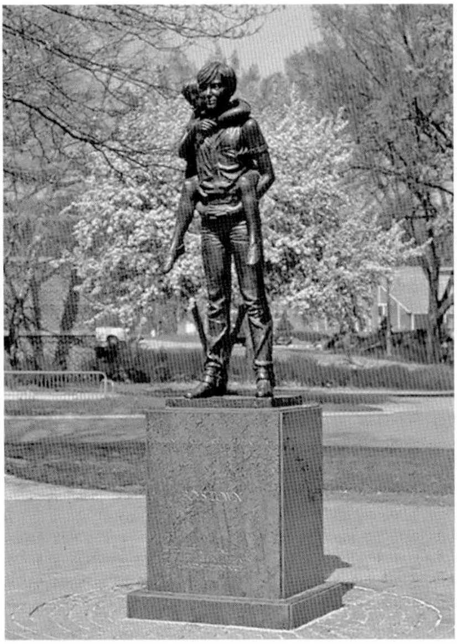

Right: Boys Town's iconic statue. *Photo courtesy Boys Town Hall of History.*

Below: Dowd Chapel at Boys Town. *Photo courtesy Boys Town Hall of History.*

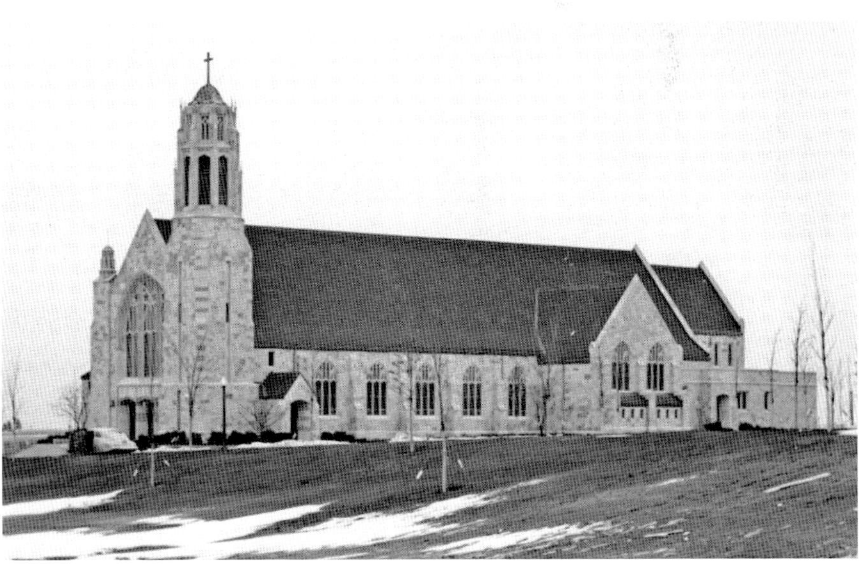

Nebraska Jewish Historical Society

333 South 132nd Street

This museum celebrating Nebraska's rich Jewish history is located in the Jewish Community Center. Its exhibits celebrate Jewish daily life, contributions to local business and religious history. It pays tribute to Jewish organizations and service to the U.S. Armed Forces. It also holds documents preserving the history of such major Omaha Jewish figures as Rose Blumkin of the Nebraska Furniture Mart; Philip Klutznick, who headed the World Jewish Congress and was a presidential cabinet member; and the J.L. Brandeis family, who founded Omaha's most important department store. Check the website for information on when it is open.[120]

Tri-Faith Center

132nd and Pacific Streets/Temple Israel

The Tri-Faith Center has attracted national attention for housing Temple Israel, American Muslim Institute and Countryside Community Church on a single campus so they can promote interfaith collaboration, education and understanding.[121] Temple Israel, Nebraska's oldest Jewish congregation, was organized in 1871. It has had several previous locations, most recently at 69th and Cass Streets.[122] Its first building at 23rd and Harney Streets was dedicated in 1884. It also formerly occupied today's St. John's Greek Orthodox Church at 602 Park Avenue.

THINGS TO DO

A revitalized Benson has become home to numerous galleries, entertainment venues, restaurants and bars. The ever-growing area that is West Omaha contains numerous shopping and eating areas, movie theaters, coffeehouses and bars as well as the traditional commercial areas of Millard and Elkhorn.

9
OUR FAVORITE SURPRISES

Before writing this book, we thought we knew Omaha. Ha!

Researching this book during the COVID-19 pandemic that closed most attractions was especially challenging, so we took to the streets, literally. After studying the history of the city's development and downloading lists of state historic markers, local buildings in the National Register of Historic Places and Omaha landmarks, we divided the city into the sectors that we feature in chapters. From driving around, we found places we hadn't known existed and developed our suggested tour routes.

We stopped to walk portions of the routes, as we suggest readers do, and discovered historic gems we were unfamiliar with in addition to learning the history of buildings we had passed without a second glance. Our city's history came alive for us in remarkable ways as we hope it will for you. You might even learn about your own neighborhoods as we did.

There's general agreement on Omaha's major attractions, like the Henry Doorly Zoo & Aquarium and the Old Market—the places where you automatically take out-of-town visitors. However we urge you to check out some of our less known favorite places, including restaurants in each sector that we especially enjoy.

PLACES TO EXPLORE

1. **Historic North 24th Street**: This area has undergone major restoration and includes such attractions as the Great Plains Black History Museum, the Union for Contemporary Arts and Dreamland Plaza, all within blocks of each other.
2. **Historic Cemeteries**, especially **Prospect Hill, Forest Lawn/Potter's Field** and **Holy Sepulchre**: All contain elaborate grave sites of the people who made Omaha. Walk through them and study the names. If you have any ties to Creighton (as both of us do), walk through the Jesuit graves adjacent to the Creighton family memorial and find the Jesuits you know in order of their deaths.
3. **Hanscom Park/Ford Birth Site**: These two adjacent sites offer one of the most beautiful walks in Omaha. They evoke the Gilded Age, when the area was one of the first suburbs. Hanscom Park includes the city's greenhouses.
4. **South 24th Street Business District**: This area speaks to both our immigrant past and our vibrant Hispanic community. It is a living display of Hispanic culture, with music, colorful wall murals, wonderful local Mexican restaurants and signs in Spanish and English. El Museo Latino just west of the business district is one of the city's finest underappreciated gems.
5. **Lewis and Clark Landing**: This Riverfront area just north of downtown where members of the Lewis and Clark Expedition camped on their famous journey will soon be the site of a major science museum. It is under construction as we write this in 2021. This spot includes lovely views of the Missouri River as well as the National Park Service Regional Office.

FUN NEIGHBORHOOD EATING SPOTS

Our apologies to the many wonderful places not listed. Our list that follows includes a single locally owned establishment in each sector that is historically significant and/or a neighborhood icon or just a place we especially like.

We could do a whole list of just beloved ice cream establishments, like Zesto's, which has several locations, or Ted & Wally's in the Old Market, where you have to line up for a block during the summer. We're omitting classic steakhouses like Johnny's in South Omaha or most new and old ethnic restaurants, classic pizza places like La Casa, craft breweries like the Upstream in the Old Market and so much more. Omaha is a city that loves to eat, so this is just a starter for places to try when you are out wandering. Bon appétit!

- **Florence**: Harold's Koffee House, 8327 North 30th Street
- **North Omaha**: Fair Deal Café, 2118 North 24th Street
- **Downtown**: Culprit Café, Brandeis Building
- **Creighton, Cathedral, Gold Coast**: Lisa's Radial Café, 817 North 40th Street
- **Dundee/Aksarben**: eCreamery Ice Cream & Gelato, 5001 Underwood Avenue
- **Near South**: La Buvette Wine & Grocery, 511 South 11th Street
- **South**: El Alamo, 4917 South 24th Street
- **Benson**: Mantra Bar & Grill, 6913 Maple Street

THINGS TO DO AT LEAST ONCE

- Tour St. Cecilia's Cathedral and walk down 38th Street past the mansions overlooking Duchesne Academy.
- Stroll through the Dundee Business District, stopping at the boutiques, eating at one of the fine small restaurants and then continue to Memorial Park for the magnificent view from the war memorial.
- Go for coffee or a drink in the newly designated historic district on South 13th Street to savor an old immigrant area gaining new life as new residents choose it for its historical ambiance and proximity to Downtown. Remember when you went to the Bohemian Café (now a brewery) as a kid and stuffed yourself on dumplings and kraut.
- Visit the Omaha Building (old Omaha National Bank) downtown and enjoy the art collection on display.
- Attend a performance at the Orpheum Theater and take extra time to explore this ornate, restored movie palace.
- Spend a weekend evening in the Blackstone or Benson districts to enjoy the new nightlife in these renovated traditional areas where Omaha has learned to reuse rather than demolish great old buildings.

CLOSING NOTE

North Omaha is Eileen's nominee for the least appreciated portion of the city. This African American area is rich in history and far from its sad traditional stereotype. Driving through the area will expose you to the investments made in upgrading old buildings and constructing new homes and businesses, to say nothing of places like Prospect Hill Cemetery and the Malcolm X Birth Site.

The same could be said of South Omaha and possibly Florence, but in most of the traditional parts of Omaha that we cover in this book, there's a mixture of old and new, restored and classic. Take some time to get to know Omaha better. We hope that you will find it fascinating and gain a new appreciation of our city as we did.

NOTES

Chapter 1

1. "Fort Omaha," Wikipedia.
2. Sorenson, *Story of Omaha*, 32.
3. Sasse, *North Omaha History* (blog), 9.
4. History Nebraska.
5. Wirth and McCabe, *Omaha's Historic Houses of Worship*, 10–13.
6. Ibid.
7. "Potter's Field (Omaha)," Wikipedia.
8. History Nebraska.
9. Ibid.
10. Official Nebraska Government Website.
11. "Keirle House," Wikipedia.
12. "Notre Dame Academy," Wikipedia.
13. "Florence Depot," Wikipedia.
14. "Mormon Bridge," Wikipedia.
15. "Florence Water Works," Wikipedia.
16. Sasse, *North Omaha History* (blog).
17. "Hummel Park," Wikipedia.

Chapter 2

18. Fogarty, *Thomas Rogers*; History Nebraska.
19. Official Nebraska Government Website.
20. "Carver Savings and Loan."
21. Author interview with Eric Ewing, April 28, 2020.
22. "History of the Jewell Building," *North Omaha History* (blog).
23. "Omaha Star Building," Wikipedia.
24. Author interview with Eric Ewing.
25. "History of the Jewell Building," *North Omaha History* (blog).
26. "Jewell Building," Wikipedia.
27. Kaufman, "Fair Deal Village MarketPlace."
28. Wirth and McCabe, *Omaha's Historic Houses of Worship*, 99.
29. Ibid., 98.
30. Ibid., 72–75.
31. "Kountze Park," Wikipedia.

Chapter 3

32. Official Nebraska Government Website.
33. Ibid.
34. Ibid.
35. Ibid.
36. Ibid.
37. "Joslyn Art Museum," Wikipedia.
38. Wirth and McCabe, *Omaha's Historic Houses of Worship*, 45–47.
39. Ibid., 22–23.
40. "Scottish Rite Cathedral," Wikipedia.
41. Fogarty, *Thomas Rogers*, 43–44.
42. Flatiron Café.
43. "Magnolia Hotel," Wikipedia.
44. "Orpheum Theatre," Wikipedia.
45. "J.L. Brandeis and Sons," Wikipedia.
46. "Omaha National Bank Building," Wikipedia.
47. "Douglas County Courthouse," Wikipedia.
48. "Lewis and Clark Landing," Visit Nebraska.
49. Omaha Parks and Recreation.

Chapter 4

50. Official Nebraska Government Website.
51. Ibid.
52. Ibid.
53. "Gold Coast Historic District," Wikipedia.
54. Fogarty, *Thomas Rogers*, 161.
55. Ibid., 222.
56. Bednarek, *Lost Omaha*, 65–66.
57. Wirth and McCabe, *Omaha's Historic Houses of Worship*, 53–62.
58. Ibid., 38.
59. Ibid., 43.
60. "Gottlieb Storz House," Wikipedia.
61. "Bemis Park Landmark," Wikipedia.
62. "History of North Omaha's," *North Omaha History*.

Chapter 5

63. Official Nebraska Government Website.
64. Ibid.
65. "Dundee Theater," Wikipedia.
66. "Dundee—Happy Hollow," Wikipedia.
67. Wirth and McCabe, *Omaha's Historic Houses of Worship*, 122.
68. Restoration Exchange Omaha.
69. Federal Writers Project, Miller, *Omaha*, 191.
70. Wirth and McCabe, *Omaha's Historic Houses of Worship*, 123.
71. "Memorial Park," Wikipedia.
72. Pospisil, "Omaha's Historic Golf Courses."
73. Federal Writers Project, Miller, *Omaha*, 192–3.
74. Bednarek, *Lost Omaha*, 33–41.
75. Ibid., 42–43.
76. Ibid., 44.
77. Ibid., 45–47.
78. Ibid., 47–49.
79. Ibid., 194.
80. Federal Writers Project, Miller, *Omaha*, 194–5.
81. Ibid.

Chapter 6

82. Official Nebraska Government Website.
83. "Field Club," Wikipedia.
84. "Ford Conservation Center," History Nebraska; "Gerald R. Ford Birthsite Gardens," Wikipedia.
85. Cole, "Omaha's Little Bohemia."
86. "Sokol Auditorium," Wikipedia.
87. "Hanscom Park," Wikipedia.
88. Wirth and McCabe, *Omaha's Historic Houses of Worship*, 51.
89. Ibid., 37.
90. Union Pacific Railroad.
91. Wirth, *Omaha's Henry Doorly Zoo*, 17–18.
92. Ibid., 19–21.
93. Ibid.
94. "Union Station," Wikipedia.
95. "Durham Museum," Wikipedia.
96. Ibid.
97. Phipps, "Market Dies."
98. Frisbie, "Old Market Turns."

Chapter 7

99. "South Omaha Nebraska," Wikipedia.
100. Official Nebraska Government Website.
101. "Vinton Street Commercial Historic," Wikipedia.
102. "South Omaha Nebraska," Wikipedia.
103. Bednarek, *Lost Omaha*, 73–75.
104. "El Museo Latino," Wikipedia.
105. "Mount Vernon Gardens," *Nebraska Realty* (blog).
106. "Brown Park," Wikipedia.
107. "South Omaha Veterans Memorial," Wikipedia.
108. "Immaculate Conception Church," Wikipedia.
109. Wirth and McCabe, *Omaha's Historic Houses of Worship*, 118.
110. Ibid., 91.
111. Ibid., 111, 113.
112. Federal Writers Project, Miller, *Omaha*, 179.

Chapter 8

113. Official Nebraska Government Website.
114. Ibid.
115. Ibid.
116. Ibid.
117. "Benson Neighborhood," Wikipedia.
118. "Krug Park," Wikipedia.
119. Boys Town.
120. Nebraska Jewish Historical Society, "Exhibits."
121. Wirth and McCabe, *Omaha's Historic Houses of Worship*, 124–25.
122. Ibid., 88–89.

BIBLIOGRAPHY

Websites

"Bemis Park Landmark Heritage District." Wikipedia. https://en.wikipedia.org/wiki/Bemis_Park_Landmark_Heritage_District.

"Benson Neighborhood." Wikipedia. https://en.wikipedia.org/wiki/Benson,_Nebraska.

Boys Town. https://www.boystown.org.

"Brown Park." Wikipedia. https://en.wikipedia/Brown_Park.

"Carver Savings and Loan Association." Wikipedia. https://en.wikipedia.org.wiki/Carver_Savings_and_Loan_Association.

"Douglas County Courthouse." Wikipedia. https://en.wikipedia.org/wiki/Douglas_County_Courthouse.

"Dundee—Happy Hollow Historic District." Wikipedia. https://en.wikipedia.org/wiki/Dundee-Happy Hollow_Historic_District."

"Dundee Theater." Wikipedia. https://en.wikipedia.org/wiki/Dundee_Theater.

"Durham Museum." Wikipedia. https://en.wikipedia.org/wiki/Durham_Museum.

"El Museo Latino." Wikipedia. https://en.wikipedia.org/wiki/El_Museo_Latino.

"Field Club." Wikipedia. http://en.wikipedia.org/Field_Club_Omaha_Nebraska.

Flatiron Café. www.flatironcafeomaha.com.

"Florence Depot." Wikipedia. https://en.wikipedia.org/wiki/Florence_Depot.
"Florence Firehouse." Wikipedia. https://en.wikipedia.org/wiki/Florence_Firehouse.
"Florence Water Works." Wikipedia. https://en.wikipedia.org/wiki/Florence_Water_Works.
"Fort Omaha." Wikipedia. https://en.wikipedia.org/wiki/Fort_Omaha.
"Gerald R. Ford Birthsite Gardens." Wikipedia. https://en.wikipedia.org/wiki/Gerald_R_Ford_Birthsite_Gardens.
"Gold Coast Historic District." Wikipedia. https://en.wikipedia.org/wiki/Gold_Coast_Historic_District(Omaha).
"Golden Spike." Wikipedia. https://en.wikipedia.org/Golden_spike.
"Gottlieb Storz House." Wikipedia. https://en.wikipedia.org/Gottlieb_Storz_House.
"Hanscom Park." Wikipedia. https://en.wikipedia.org/wiki/Hanscom_Park.
History Nebraska. https://history.nebraska.gov.
"A History of the Jewell Building and Dreamland Ballroom." *North Omaha History* (blog). https://northomahahistory.com.
"A History of North Omaha's Walnut Hill Reservoir." *North Omaha History* (blog). https://northomahahistory.com.
"Hummel Park." Wikipedia. htps://en.wikipedia.org/wiki/Hummel_Park.
"Immaculate Conception Church." Wikipedia. https://en.wikipedia.org/Immaculate_Conception_Church.
"Jewell Building." Wikipedia. https://en.wikipedia.org/wiki/Jewell_Building.
"J.L. Brandeis and Sons Store." Wikipedia. https://en.wikipedia.org/wiki/J_L_Brandeis_and_Sons_Store.
"Joslyn Art Museum." Wikipedia. http://en.wikipedia.org/wiki/Joslyn_Art_Museum.
"Keirle House." Wikipedia. https://en.wikipedia.org/wiki/Keirle_House.
"Kountze Park." Wikipedia. https://en.wikipedia.org/wiki/Kountze_Park_(Omaha_Nebraska).
"Krug Park." Wikipedia. https://en.wikipedia.org/wiki/Krug_Park_(amusement_park).
"Lewis and Clark Landing." Visit Nebraska. https://visitnebraska.com/omaha/lewis-and-clark-landing.
"Magnolia Hotel." Wikipedia. http://en.wikipedia.org/wiki/Magnolia_Hotel_(Omaha).

"Memorial Park." Wikipedia. https://en.wikipedia.org/wiki/Memorial_Park.
"Mormon Bridge." Wikipedia. https://en.wikipedia.org/wiki/Mormon_Bridge_(Omaha).
"Mount Vernon Gardens, Omaha Nebraska." *Nebraska Realty* (blog). nebraskarealtyonline.com/our-community/mount-vernon-gardens.
Nebraska Jewish Historical Society. "Exhibits." https://nebraskajhs.com/home/exhibits.
"Notre Dame Academy and Convent." Wikipedia. https://en.wikipedia.org/wiki/Notre_Dame_Academy_and_Convent.
7Official Nebraska Government Website. Nebraska State Historical Society. http://www.e-nebraskahistory.org/index.php?title=Main_Page.
"Omaha National Bank Building." Wikipedia. https://en.wikipedia.org/wiki/Omaha_National_Bank_Building).
Omaha Parks and Recreation. https://parks.cityofomaha.org.
"Omaha Star Building." Wikipedia. https://en.wikipedia.org/wiki/Omaha_Star_building.
"Orpheum Theatre." Wikipedia. http://en.wikipedia.org/wiki/Orpheum_Theatre_(Omaha).
"Potter's Field (Omaha)." Wikipedia. https://en.wikipedia.org/wiki/Potter's_Field_(Omaha).
Restoration Exchange Omaha. https://www.restorationexchange.org.
"Rose Blumkin Performing Arts Center." Wikipedia. https://en.wikipedia.org/wiki/Rose_Blumkin_Performing_Arts_Center.
Sasse, Adam Fletcher. *North Omaha History* (blog). https://northomahahistory.com.
"Scottish Rite Cathedral." Wikipedia. https://en.wikipedia.org/wiki/Scottish_Rite_Cathedral_(Omaha).
"Sokol Auditorium." Wikipedia. https://en.wikipedia.org/wiki/Sokol_Auditorium.
"South Omaha Main Street Historic." Wikipedia. https://en.wikipedia.org/wiki/South_Omaha_Main_Street_Historic.
"South Omaha Nebraska." Wikipedia. https://en.wikipedia.org/wiki/South_Omaha_Nebraska.
"South Omaha Veterans Memorial." Wikipedia. https://en.wikipedia/South_Omaha_Veterans_Memorial.
Union Pacific Railroad. https://www.up.com/index.htm.
"Union Station." Wikipedia. https://en.wikipedia.org/wiki/Union_Station_(Omaha).

"Vinton Street Commercial Historic." Wikipedia. https://en.wikipedia.org/wiki/Vinton_Street_Commercial_Historic.

Tourist Information

Mormon Pioneer National Trail, U.S. National Park Service.

Interviews

Martin Shukert, June 4, 2020.

Books

Bednarek, Janet R. Daly. *Lost Omaha*. Charleston, SC: The History Press, 2018.

Chatelain, Dirk. *24th and Glory*. Omaha, NE: *Omaha World-Herald*, 2019.

Federal Writers Project, Linda Miller, ed. and index. *Omaha: A Guide to the City and Environs*. Omaha, NE: Omaha Public Library, 1981.

Fogarty, Joan. *Thomas Rogers Kimball*. Omaha, NE: N.p, 2019.

Reiner, Kim. *Lost Restaurants of Omaha*. Charleston, SC: The History Press, 2017.

Schlesinger, Arthur M., Jr. *Robert Kennedy and His Times*. Boston: Houghton Mifflin, 1978.

Sorenson, Alfred. *The Story of Omaha*. 3rd ed. Omaha, NE: National Printing Company, 1923.

Werthman, Ione, ed. *St. Cecilia's Cathedral*. Omaha, NE: St. Cecilia's Cathedral, 1980.

Wirth, Eileen. *Omaha's Henry Doorly Zoo & Aquarium*. Charleston, SC: The History Press, 2017.

Wirth, Eileen, and Carol McCabe. *Omaha's Historic Houses of Worship*. Charleston, SC: Arcadia Publishing, 2014.

Newspaper Articles

Cole, Kevin. "Omaha's Little Bohemia Added to the National Register of Historic Places." Omaha.com, July 27, 2020.

Frisbie, Al. "Old Market Turns Some Dreams into Reality." *Omaha World-Herald*, January 14,1968.

Omaha World Herald. "Hansen Heron Haven Sanctuary." January 4, 2015. https://omaha.com/sports/local-sports/hansen-heron-haven-sanctuary.

Phipps, Robert. "Market Dies and so Does and Era." *Omaha World-Herald*, January 15, 1964.

Pospisil, Stu. "Omaha's Historic Golf Courses Lie Beneath the City We See Today." Omaha.com, April 26, 2020.

Magazine Articles

Horan, Judy. "Bombs Bursting in Air." *Omaha Magazine*, September 15, 2014.

Kaufman, Kirby. "Fair Deal Village MarketPlace." *Omaha Magazine*, August 23, 2017.

"Krug Park." *Omaha Magazine*, April 28, 2015.

INDEX

ABOUT THE AUTHORS

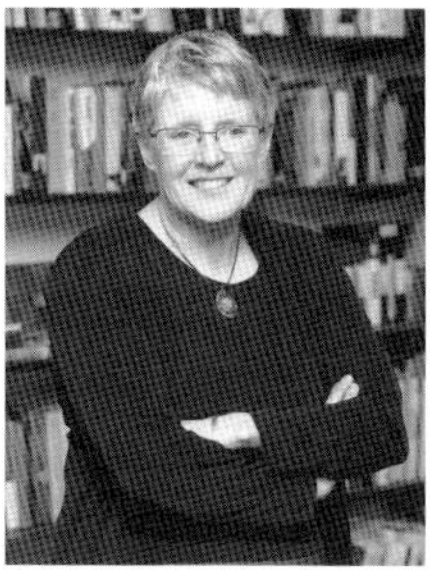

Dr. Eileen Wirth is a professor emeritus of journalism at Creighton University and is an author specializing in Omaha history. She was a reporter at the *World-Herald* and a PR writer for Union Pacific before joining Creighton in 1991.

Eileen's books include *The Henry Doorly Zoo & Aquarium*, *Historic Omaha Houses of Worship* (both with Carol McCabe) and *From Society Page to Front Page*. She is on the board of History Nebraska has been active in numerous groups, particularly the Omaha Public Library.

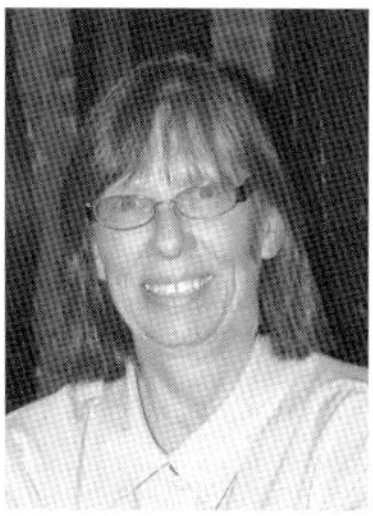

Carol McCabe has worked in all areas of photography, including owning a traditional photo lab, running a photography gallery in Omaha's Old Market district, working in photographic archives and serving as photo editor for various publications.